# Jack and the Giant

## A Family Musical

## David Wood

A SAMUEL FRENCH ACTING EDITION

# SAMUEL FRENCH

FOUNDED 1830

SAMUELFRENCH-LONDON.CO.UK
SAMUELFRENCH.COM

ISBN 978-0-573-05080-0

www.samuelfrench-london.co.uk

www.samuelfrench.com

---

## FOR AMATEUR PRODUCTION ENQUIRIES

### UNITED KINGDOM AND WORLD
### EXCLUDING NORTH AMERICA
plays@SamuelFrench-London.co.uk
### 020 7255 4302/01

Each title is subject to availability from Samuel French,

depending upon country of performance.

---

## JACK AND THE GIANT

Jack and the Giant was first produced at the Queen's Theatre, Hornchurch, on 6th December, 1982, with the following cast of characters:

| | |
|---|---|
| **Mrs Macdonald** | John Halstead |
| **Jack Mac** | David Learner |
| **Jeannie Mac** | Patience Tomlinson |
| **Dog** | Penny Jones |
| **Marigold**, a cow | Paul Aylett and Vivien Stokes |
| **Duck** | Jacqui Finch |
| **Pig** | David Nunn |
| **Mr Meany** | John Gay |
| **Sergeant Sweet** | Paul Tomany |
| **Beep** | Richard Bremmer |
| **Buzz** | Tony Kenway |
| **The Silver Giant** | Paul Tomany |
| **Baby Giant** | David Nunn |
| **Cloud Cuckoos** | Paul Aylett, Jacqui Finch, John Gay, David Nunn, Vivien Stokes, Paul Tomany |
| **Ducklings** and **Piglets** | Tina Aldridge, Tina Einchcombe, Sandra Holgate, Peter Nicholls, Andrea Poyser, Karen Wood, Kellie Chappell, Jenni Harper, Lorraine Judge, Victoria Ludlow, Paul Nicholls, Sally Ann Wright |

| | |
|---|---|
| Director | Paul Tomlinson |
| Musical Director and Arranger | Robert Davidson |
| Set and Costume Design | Ian Wilson |

## Suggested doubling for a cast of 12

M1    Mrs Macdonald
M2    Jack Mac
M3    Beep
M4    Buzz
M5    Sergeant Sweet/Cloud Cuckoo/The Silver Giant
M6    Mr Meany/Cloud Cuckoo
F1    Jeannie Mac
F2    Cow (front)/Cloud Cuckoo
F3    Cow (back)/Cloud Cuckoo
F4    Duck/Cloud Cuckoo
M/F1  Dog
M/F2  Pig/Cloud Cuckoo/Baby Giant

# CHARACTERS

| | |
|---|---|
| **Mrs Macdonald:** | warm, lovable but sharp dame character; she runs the farm |
| **Jack Mac:** | her son; not idle, just preoccupied with his dream of building a rocket—at first this leads him astray, but eventually proves he's really a winner |
| **Jeannie Mac:** | her daughter; reliable, hard-working tomboy; the practical member of the family |
| **Dog:** | the family pet who is also a working farm dog |
| **Marigold:** | a cow |
| **Mr Meany:** | a mercenary, unfair landlord |
| **Sergeant Sweet:** | a friendly policeman |
| **Beep:** | a tall, efficient spaceman |
| **Buzz:** | a short, less efficient spaceman |
| **The Silver Giant:** | a traditional, though silver, selfish giant |
| **Baby Giant:** | his son, aged no more than a year, but already taller than Jack Mac |
| **Pig:** | the mother of five piglets |
| **Piglets:** | preferably played by children of staggered heights |
| **Duck:** | the mother of five ducklings |
| **Ducklings:** | preferably played by children of staggered heights |
| **The Cloud Cuckoos:** | who live in Cloud Cuckoo land and act as a backing group for Jack |

# SYNOPSIS OF SCENES

**ACT I**

**ACT II**

## MUSICAL NUMBERS

**ACT 1**

Overture

| | | |
|---|---|---|
| 1 | **Mrs Macdonald's Farm** | Mrs Macdonald, Marigold, Dog, Pigs, Ducks, Jeannie and Audience |
| 2 | **My Rocket/Cloud Cuckoo Land** | Jack, Mrs Macdonald, Jeannie, Pigs and Ducks |
| 2A | **Fanfare** | |
| 2B | **Fanfare** | |
| 2C | **Entrance Music** | |
| 2D | **Underscore** | |
| 2E | **Tension Music** | |
| 2F | **Underscore** | |
| 3 | **Marigold** | Mrs Macdonald, Jack, (Dog), Jeannie, Pigs and Ducks |
| 3A | **Exit Music** | |
| 4 | **Beep! Buzz!** | Beep, Buzz and Audience |
| 4A | **Beep! Buzz! (Reprise)** | Beep, Buzz |
| 4B | **Entrance Music** | |
| 4C | **Incidental/**Tension | |
| 4D | **Incidental** | |
| 5 | **Keep Your Pecker Up** | Jack, (Dog), Pigs and Ducks |
| 5A | **Scene Change** | |
| 5B | **Incidental** | |
| 6 | **Sweet Dreams** | Mrs Macdonald and Audience |
| 6A | **Scene Change/Underscore/Scene Change** | |
| 6B | **Cloud Cuckoo Land** (Reprise) | Jack, (Dog), Cuckoos |

**ACT 2**

Entr'acte

| | | |
|---|---|---|
| 7 | **A Baked Bean Tin Tree** | Mrs Macdonald, Pigs and Ducks |
| 7A | **Underscore/chase** | |
| 7B | **Incidental** | |
| 7C | **Entrance/chase music** | |
| 8 | **Woof Moo-oo!** | Dog, Marigold |
| 8A | **Exit music/scene change** | |
| 8B | **Entrance music** | |
| 8C | **Entrance music** | |
| 9 | **The Silver Giant's Lament** | Silver Giant, Baby Giant, Beep, Buzz, Jack |

| 9A | **Sweet Dreams** (Reprise) | Jack, Mrs Macdonald and Audience |
|---|---|---|
| 9B | **Incidental/chase/fight music** | |
| 9C | **Entrance music** | |
| 9D | **A Baked Bean Tin Tree** (Reprise) | Mrs Macdonald, Jeannie and (Dog) |
| 9E | **Chase** | |
| 10 | **Use Your Eyes and Ears** | Sergeant Sweet, Pigs, Ducks and Audience |
| 10A | **Outer Space music** | |
| 10B | **Marigold** (Reprise) | Mrs Macdonald, Jack, Jeannie, (Dog), Pigs, Ducks |
| 10C | **Mrs Macdonald's Farm** (Reprise) | Mrs Macdonald, Jack, Jeannie, (Dog), Marigold, Pigs, Ducks |
| 10D | **Encore** | |
| 10E | **House exit** | |

# ACT I*

*Mrs Macdonald's Farmyard*

**Overture**

*After a short overture, the* Curtain *rises*

*To one side of the stage is the exterior of a small, picturesque farmhouse, complete with practical door and windows. To the other side is a small, tumbledown shack, which is used as a workshop. Near it is a dog kennel. Signposts could point "TO THE DUCKPOND" or "TO THE PIGSTY". A water pump and water-trough are visible, plus bales of straw etc. Also an animals' feeding trough. It is morning*

*Mrs Macdonald enters from the farmhouse carrying a mop and bucket. She is searching for her son*

**Mrs Macdonald** Jack! Jack!

*No sign. She puts down the bucket, then turns to the house and shouts up to a bedroom window*

Jack, are you up there? Are you *up* up there? If you're *not* up up there, I'm coming up up there to get you up up there and down down here! So there, there, there! (*She turns back and starts towards the water pump, putting her foot in the bucket as she does so. She clatters along*) Oh, dearie me. I've put me foot in it now. (*She shouts*) Jack! Will you come and help your poor old mother this minute? (*She gets the bucket off her foot and goes to the pump*) It's time you pulled your nose up and put your socks to the grindstone. Or something like that. (*She starts pumping water*) We've got all those people coming to visit the farm today. They'll be here soon, so I need your h—— (*She suddenly notices the audience and does a huge double-take, before stammering*)—h . . . h . . . h . . . HELP! They're here already. (*She calls "aside"*) Jack! (*She puts down the bucket, tries to smarten herself up; then approaches the audience*) Good-morning.
**Audience** Good-morning.
**Mrs Macdonald** GOOD-MORNING.
**Audience** GOOD-MORNING.
**Mrs Macdonald** GOOD-MOR . . . NING.

---

*N.B. Paragraph 3 on page ii of this Acting Edition regarding photocopying and video-recording should be carefully read.

**Audience** GOOD-MOR ... NING.

**Mrs Macdonald** What are you doing here? I mean, you're early. I mean, you're not meant to be here yet. I mean, you're ... you're ... (*pulling herself together*) ... you're *very* welcome. I'm Mrs Macdonald. Mrs Mac for short. Mrs April May June Julia Augusta Macdonald for long. Who are you? Come on, shout your names out!

*The audience do so. Mrs Macdonald repeats a few, saying "Hallo"*

Have any of you been on a farm before?

*She encourages the audience to call out*

Well, whether you have or not, today we're going to show you who lives on our farm and what we all do. (*She calls*) Jack!

*No reply. Mrs Macdonald shrugs and goes into her song*

### Song 1: Mrs Macdonald's Farm

(*Singing*)          I'm Mrs Macdonald
                     And this is my farm

*The audience should be encouraged to join in the refrains, plus the animal noises*

                     E I E I O
                     And on my farm I have a dog—

*Fanfare*

*Dog enters from his kennel. He barks in the appropriate places, encouraging the audience to join in*

                     E I E I O
                     With a (*bark bark*) here
                     A (*bark bark*) there
                     Here a (*bark*)
                     There a (*bark*)
                     Ev'rywhere a (*bark*)
                     I'm Mrs Macdonald
                     And this is my farm
                     E I E I O

*The music continues*

(*Speaking*) What other animals do you think I've got?

*The audience shout out suggestions. Dog and Mrs Macdonald pick up a few and pretend to hear a few exotic ones*

A camel? No! Rhinocerosisisizz? No! I'll show you ...

(*Singing*)          I'm Mrs Macdonald
                     And this is my farm
                     E I E I O
                     And on my farm I have a cow—

*Fanfare. Dog beckons in:*

*A Cow, who does a quick couple of dance steps, then moos*

> E I E I O
> With a (*moo moo*) here
> A (*moo moo*) there
> Here a (*moo*)
> There a (*moo*)
> Ev'rywhere a (*moo*)
> With a (*bark bark*) here
> A (*bark bark*) there
> Here a (*bark*)
> There a (*bark*)
> Ev'rywhere a (*bark*)
> I'm Mrs Macdonald
> And this is my farm
> E I E I O
> I'm Mrs Macdonald
> And this is my farm
> E I E I O
> And on my farm I have a daughter—

*Fanfare*

*Jeannie enters, pushing a wheelbarrow full of logs*

*The music continues*

(*Speaking*) This is Jeannie. Jeannie Mac. What have you been doing, dearie?

**Jeannie** Chopping logs, Mum.

**Mrs Macdonald** Dearie me. Your brother should've done that. Girls can't chop logs. (*To the audience*) Can they?

**Audience** (*led by Jeannie*) Yes.

**Mrs Macdonald** Oh no they can't.

**Audience** Oh yes they can.

**Mrs Macdonald** Oh no they can't.

**Audience** Oh yes they can.

**Mrs Macdonald** Just checking.

**Jeannie** I enjoyed it.

**Mrs Macdonald** Thank you, dearie.
(*Singing*)        E I E I O

*Jeannie sings doing the actions—the Cow and Dog join in*

**Jeannie**        With a chop chop here
            A chop chop there
            Here a chop
            There a chop
            Ev'rywhere a chop
**All**        With a (*moo moo*) here

|                   | A *(moo moo)* there |
|-------------------|---------------------|
|                   | Here a *(moo)* |
|                   | There a *(moo)* |
|                   | Ev'rywhere a *(moo)* |
|                   | With a *(bark bark)* here |
|                   | A *(bark bark)* there |
|                   | Here a *(bark)* |
|                   | There a *(bark)* |
|                   | Ev'rywhere a *(bark)* |
| **Mrs Macdonald** | I'm Mrs Macdonald |
|                   | And this is my farm |
| **All**           | E I E I O |
| **Mrs Macdonald** | I'm Mrs Macdonald |
|                   | And this is my farm |
| **All**           | E I E I O |
| **Mrs Macdonald** | And on my farm I have some ducks— |

*Fanfare*

*A Duck enters with her Ducklings in line behind her. They do a short duck dance*

|                   | |
|-------------------|---------------------|
| **All**           | E I E I O |
|                   | With a *(quack quack)* here |
|                   | A *(quack quack)* there |
|                   | Here a *(quack)* |
|                   | There a *(quack)* |
|                   | Ev'rywhere a *(quack)* |
|                   | With a chop chop here |
|                   | A chop chop there |
|                   | Here a chop |
|                   | There a chop |
|                   | Ev'rywhere a chop |
| **All**           | With a *(moo moo)* here |
|                   | A *(moo moo)* there |
|                   | Here a *(moo)* |
|                   | There a *(moo)* |
|                   | Ev'rywhere a *(moo)* |
|                   | With a *(bark bark)* here |
|                   | A *(bark bark)* there |
|                   | Here a *(bark)* |
|                   | There a *(bark)* |
|                   | Ev'rywhere a *(bark)* |
| **Mrs Macdonald** | I'm Mrs Macdonald |
|                   | And this is my farm |
| **All**           | E I E I O |
| **Mrs Macdonald** | I'm Mrs Macdonald |
|                   | And this is my farm |
| **All**           | E I E I O |
| **Mrs Macdonald** | And on my farm I have some pigs— |

*Fanfare*

*A Pig enters followed by Piglets. They do a short pig dance*

**All**                E I E I O
                       With a (*snort snort*) here
                       A (*snort snort*) there
                       Here a (*snort*)
                       There a (*snort*)
                       Ev'rywhere a (*snort*)
                       With a (*quack quack*) here
                       A (*quack quack*) there
                       Here a (*quack*)
                       There a (*quack*)
                       Ev'rywhere a (*quack*)
                       With a chop chop here
                       A chop chop there
                       Here a chop
                       There a chop
                       Ev'rywhere a chop
**All**                With a (*moo moo*) here
                       A (*moo moo*) there
                       Here a (*moo*)
                       There a (*moo*)
                       Ev'rywhere a (*moo*)
                       With a (*bark bark*) here
                       A (*bark bark*) there
                       Here a (*bark*)
                       There a (*bark*)
                       Ev'rywhere a (*bark*)
**Mrs Macdonald**      I'm Mrs Macdonald
                       And this is my farm
**All**                E I E I O
**Jeannie** Breakfast time!

*The animals make excited anticipatory noises. Jeannie hands her mother a basket of grain*

**Mrs Macdonald** Dearie me. Jack should be helping. Here you are, ducks.

*They peck from her hand*

   Where is he, Jeannie?
**Jeannie** (*tipping a large bucket of yucky pigswill into the feeding trough*) No idea, Mum. Come and get it, pigs!

*The Pigs tuck in. Jeannie gives some hay to the Cow. Dog stays near the Cow*

**Mrs Macdonald** Let's give him a shout. (*She has an idea*) Maybe our visitors would like to help. (*To the audience*) Would you?
**Audience** Yes!
**Mrs Macdonald** Would you help us call for Jack?

**Audience** Yes!
**Mrs Macdonald** Thank you. After three then. (*Demonstrating*) Jack
  Ma——ac! One, two, three.
**All** Jack Ma——ac!

*No reaction*

**Mrs Macdonald** A little louder? One, two three.
**All** Jack Ma—ac!

*No reaction*

**Mrs Macdonald** Once more. One, two three.
**All** Jack Ma—ac!

> *Jack enters from the tumbledown shack. He wears spectacles and carries a
> large sheet of paper—a set of plans—which he studies intently*

> *Unseen by Mrs Macdonald, who is facing front, he wanders downstage, not
> looking where he is going. He bumps into Mrs Macdonald*

**Mrs Macdonald** Aaaaah! (*She does a huge reaction*)
**Jack** (*calmly*) Hallo, Mum.
**Mrs Macdonald** Don't you "hallo, Mum" me!
**Jack** Oh. Goodbye, Mum. (*He wanders off*)
**Mrs Macdonald** Come back, Jack Mac. Where have you been?
**Jack** In the shack, Mum.
**Mrs Macdonald** In the shack, Jack Mac?
**Jack** In the shack.
**Mrs Macdonald** And now you're back from the shack, Jack Mac?
**Jack** Yes.
**Mrs Macdonald** Well, I've got something for you.
**Jack** Oh. What, Mum?
**Mrs Macdonald** A smack, Jack Mac, a dirty great smack ... you great
  pudd'n'.

> *She goes for him. Jeannie intervenes*

**Jeannie** Break it up you two.
**Jack** Jeannie, can I borrow that bucket?
**Jeannie** What for?
**Jack** I could use it for my ... what I'm making.
**Jeannie** What are you making, Jack?
**Jack** (*shyly*) A rocket.
**Jeannie** A rocket?
**Mrs Macdonald** I'll give you a rocket. You great pudd'n'.
**Jeannie** What kind of rocket?
**Jack** A space rocket.
**Jeannie** (*amazed, not dismissive*) You're making a space rocket? In that
  shack?
**Jack** Yes. Look.

> *He shows her his plans. The animals look too*

**Song 2: My Rocket/Cloud Cuckoo Land**

(*Singing*)        My rocket
This is my rocket
My fly me high in the sky rocket
I'll be off to the moon
Soon
My rocket
This is my rocket
My DIY do or die rocket
Just you wait and see
With pace and grace
We'll race through space
My rocket
And me.

*The music continues under*

(*Speaking*) What do you think?
**Jeannie** I think it's amazing.
**Jack** Mum?
**Mrs Macdonald** I can see it all now. On launching day. All the important people, the dignifaries ... the difnitig ... the digitnigit ... the nobs—coming up to me—standing there in me best wellies, with tears in my eyes—and saying "Mrs Macdonald, you must be the mother of Jack Mac, that *great* ..."
**Jack** (*carried away*) Scientist?
**Mrs Macdonald** "Pudd'n'! That great pudd'n'!"

(*Singing*)        You've got your
Head in the clouds
Your feet off the ground
Your nose in the air
You've got your
Head in the clouds
You seem
To live in a dream.

(*Speaking*) You're living in Cloud Cuckoo Land.
**Jack** What's that?
**Mrs Macdonald** Cloud Cuckoo Land? There's no such place! Except in your head!

(*Singing*)        Cloud Cuckoo Land is for cuckoos
Cuckoos who don't know what's what
Cloud Cuckoo Land
May seem grand
To you
But I can assure you it's not.

Cloud Cuckoo Land is for dreamers

Dreamers who get nothing done
Cloud Cuckoo Land
Understand
Is not
The land for the likes of my son.

*They sing in counterpoint. If required, the animals and Jeannie could join in—*
*Jeannie singing with Jack and the Ducks, Mrs Macdonald singing with the*
*Pigs*

| **Jack** | **Mrs Macdonald** |
|---|---|
| My rocket | Cloud Cuckoo Land is for cuckoos |
| This is my rocket | Cuckoos who don't know what's what |
| | Cloud Cuckoo Land |
| My fly me high in the sky | May seem grand |
|   rocket | To you |
| I'll be off to the moon | But I can assure you it's not. |
| | Cloud Cuckoo Land is for dreamers |
| Soon | Dreamers who get nothing done |
| My rocket | Cloud Cuckoo Land |
| My rocket | Understand |
| This is my rocket | Is not |
| | The land for the likes of my son. |
| My DIY do or die rocket | Cloud Cuckoo Land is for cuckoos |
| | Cuckoos who don't know what's what |
| Just you wait and see | Cloud Cuckoo Land |
| | May seem grand |
| With pace and grace | To you |
| | But I can assure you it's not. |
| We'll race through space | Cloud Cuckoo Land is for dreamers |
| | Dreamers who get nothing done |
| My rocket | Cloud Cuckoo Land |
| | Understand |
| And me. | Is not |
| | The land for the likes of my son. |

**Jack**           With my rocket
                     The world's in my pocket
**Mrs Macdonald**  I beg to disagree
**Jack**          You'll see!
                     My rocket and me.

*Jack sets off back to the shack*

**Mrs Macdonald** Jack! Where are you off to?
**Jack** Back to the shack.
**Mrs Macdonald** You can't. We've got all these visitors—(*indicating the audience*)—to show round the farm.
**Jack** Maybe they'd like to see my rocket.
**Mrs Macdonald** Of course not. (*To the audience*) You don't want to see his rocket, do you?

**Audience** Yes!
**Mrs Macdonald** Oh no you don't.
**Audience** Oh yes we do.
**Mrs Macdonald** Oh no you don't.
**Audience** Oh yes we do.
**Mrs Macdonald** Don't!
**Audience** Do!
**Mrs Macdonald** Just checking. (*To Jack*) For some reason what I know not why, they want to see your rocket.
**Jack** Oh. Er ... well ... you see ... er ...
**Mrs Macdonald** Come on. It was your idea. Don't shilly shally. Show 'em your rocket.
**Jack** I can't ...
**Mrs Macdonald** What?
**Jack** Yet. It's not finished.
**Mrs Macdonald** Well, you'd better finish it a bit sharpish. They're only here a couple of hours, you know. Not bed and breakfast.
**Jack** Yes, Mum.

*He disappears into the shack, taking Jeannie's bucket*

**Jeannie** I'd better go and mow the barley meadow.
**Mrs Macdonald** All right, dearie.
**Jeannie** I'll take Dog.
**Mrs Macdonald** Why?
**Jeannie** Like the song. (*She sings*) "One man went to mow, went to mow a meadow."

*Mrs Macdonald joins in*

**Both** "One man and his dog, went to mow a meadow."
**Jeannie** Come on, Dog.

*Dog starts to go*

**Mrs Macdonald** (*suddenly*) Wait a tick. Jack should be doing that. Like in the song. One *man* and his dog ...
**Jeannie** Oh, Mum, it's all right, really.
**Mrs Macdonald** But you'll have to drive the combine harvester. (*To the audience*) Girls can't drive combine harvesters, can they?
**Audience** Yes.
**Mrs Macdonald** Oh no they can't.
**Audience** Oh yes they can.
**Mrs Macdonald** Just checking.
**Jeannie** See you later.

*Jeannie and Dog exit*

**Mrs Macdonald** Now then, what's next? (*To the audience*) Oh, yes. It's time to demonstrate to you "How to milk a cow." Would you like that?
**Audience** Yes.

**Mrs Macdonald** Mm. I thought so. (*She goes to the Cow*) Well, Jack usually milks the cow, but I suppose I'll have to do it today. This is Marigold.

### Music 2A: Fanfare

*Marigold bows*

Marigold will assist me in the demonstration.

*Marigold shakes her head*

Why not?

*Marigold whispers in Mrs Macdonald's ear*

I haven't got cold hands.

*Marigold nods*

*The Ducks and Pigs start making laughing noises*

What are you lot gawping at? Go on. Hop it. Back to your pond, ducks. Pigs, back to your sty.

*The animals exit*

Now then. "How to milk a cow."

### Music 2B: Fanfare

*Mrs Macdonald fetches a stool and a bucket. If necessary she could read from a list of instructions*

One. "Place cow in suitable position." Right, Marigold. Over here. So everyone can see.

*She leads Marigold c, then turns back to the audience or her list*

Good. Now then ... Two.

*Marigold has straightaway moved to one side, behind Mrs Macdonald's line of vision. The audience should shout out*

Here we are. (*Noticing the audience*) What? Marigold's what? (*Seeing her*) You naughty girl. Come back here. (*She leads her back, then turns away*) Good. Two ...

*Marigold moves again. Same routine. The Audience shout out*

What? (*Seeing*) Oh, she's at it again. Marigold, you cheeky cow. Come back here.

*This time Mrs Macdonald stands close to Marigold so that she cannot move*

Two. "Sit on stool." Well, that's easy enough.

*Marigold promptly sits on the stool*

Where is it? (*Searching*) It was here a moment ago. (*Calling*) Stoo—ool!

*The audience shout out that Marigold is sitting on it*

*(Hearing the audience)* She's what? *(Seeing)* Marigold. Stand up.

*Marigold stands. Mrs Macdonald faces front again*

Right. Two. "Sit on stool." Here goes.

*Marigold niftily sits on the stool. Straightaway Mrs Macdonald sits, ending up on Marigold's lap*

Aaaaaah! *(She struggles up)* Get up, you cheeky cow. *I* sit on the stool, not you.

*Marigold stands. Mrs Macdonald goes to sit daintily on the stool. Marigold kicks it from under her. Mrs Macdonald sits on the ground*

Aaaaaah! Marigold, behave. *(She gets up, and replaces the stool)* Stop showing off.

*She goes to sit again, and again Marigold kicks it from under her. Mrs Macdonald sits on the ground*

Aaaaaah! *(She rubs her bottom)* Ow. I sat upon my sit upon. *(She grabs the stool and sits on it)* Now. *(Returning to her list, or simply facing front)* Three. "Place bucket under cow." Bucket.

*The bucket is too far away to pick up without getting up from the stool. She starts to get up, thinks better of it, and walks in a sitting position holding on to the stool behind her. Marigold follows. Mrs Macdonald picks up the bucket and continues in a circle to return to square one. Marigold follows close behind. Mrs Macdonald can't see Marigold*

*(Calling)* Marigold! Where are you. Don't muck about.

*The audience should shout "She's behind you", but wherever Mrs Macdonald goes (still in her stool-squatting position), Marigold follows close behind. Mrs Macdonald stops. Marigold bumps into her back, knocking her over in such a way that she gets the bucket stuck on her head*

Aaaaaah! *(She leaves the stool on the ground as she struggles to get the bucket off. She does so, and staggers around dazed. She sees Marigold)* This is your last chance, Marigold. Stay still.

*Marigold makes a small movement*

Still!

*Marigold's movements become less and less with each "Still".*

Still! Still! Still! Still! Still! Good girl.

*Marigold is still, and in the right position. Mrs Macdonald sets up the stool and the bucket, but does so without taking her eyes off Marigold. Because of this she carefully muddles up the stool and the bucket—placing the stool under Marigold . . .*

Bucket under cow.

*... and the bucket alongside*

Stool. Fine. Sit on stool. (*She daintily sits in the bucket*) Aaaaaaah! (*She gets up and runs around with the bucket stuck on her bottom*)

*Marigold "laughs". Eventually Mrs Macdonald manages to remove the bucket*

Bucket. (*She places it under Marigold*) Stool. (*She places the stool in the proper place. She sits*) Four. "Tug teats."

*Marigold moos with fright*

Quiet, Marigold. Now, where are your teats? I've got to tug 'em.

*Marigold tries to hide her udders by crossing her legs and crouching. Mrs Macdonald delves. Marigold moos as though tickled*

I won't tickle you, you silly cow. Come on. Don't be shy.

*Marigold allows herself to be touched, tensing up in anticipation*

Five. "After five tugs, stand by for squirt-off." Ready, Marigold?

*Marigold nods nervously*

(*To the audience*) Ready everyone?
**Audience** Yes.
**Mrs Macdonald** (*tugging teats, encouraging the audience to join in the countdown*) Five, four, three, two, one——

*Bang! An explosion from the shack interrupts the milking. Marigold bolts. Mrs Macdonald falls off her stool*

*The Ducks and the Pigs hurry on to see what has happened*

*Smoke emerges from the shack. The door opens and Jack staggers out. His face is blackened and his clothes somewhat tattered. He carries a bent and battered bucket*

**Jack** Sorry, Mum. Technical hitch.
**Mrs Macdonald** I thought rockets were meant to go up not blow up. Are you all right, dearie?

*Mrs Macdonald, Marigold, the Ducks and Pigs surround Jack to help him recover. They all stand in a huddle on one side of the stage*

### Music 2C: Sinister Entrance Music

*From the other side of the stage, unseen by Mrs Macdonald and Co., Mr Meany enters. He looks covetously at the farmhouse, rubs his hands, then beckons to someone off-stage. Sergeant Sweet enters. Mr Meany points to Mrs Macdonald and pushes Sergeant Sweet towards her. Sergeant Sweet coughs*

**Sergeant Sweet** Excuse me, madam.

*Mrs Macdonald and the others turn, surprised*

**Mrs Macdonald** Oh. I'm so sorry. I didn't see you, Constable.

**Sergeant Sweet** (*proudly*) Sergeant actually, madam.

**Mrs Macdonald** Oh. Congratulations. *Sergeant.* (*She curtsies*)

**Sergeant Sweet** Sweet.

**Mrs Macdonald** I beg your pudd'n'?

**Sergeant Sweet** Sweet.

**Mrs Macdonald** (*giving him a playful slap*) Flatterer. You're pretty tasty yourself.

**Sergeant Sweet** Sweet be my *name*, madam.

**Mrs Macdonald** I *see*. Sweet by name, sweet by nature, I bet.

**Sergeant Sweet** (*pleasantly embarrassed*) Well, I er ...

**Mr Meany** Will you get on with it, Sergeant?

*He has been sheltering behind Sergeant Sweet, but now emerges and is seen by Mrs Macdonald and the others*

**Mrs Macdonald** Oh, it's Mr Meany.

*Chorus of disparaging moos, boos and snorts from the animals*

(*To the audience*) Meany by name, meany by nature. (*With a phoney smile*) Good Meany, Mr Morning ... I mean morning, Mr Meany.

**Mr Meany** (*with an oily leer*) A good morning indeed, dear lady; for *me*.

**Mrs Macdonald** You know my son Jack? He's just given me a nasty rock with his shocket ... I mean shock with his rocket.

**Mr Meany** How distressing for you, dear lady, to have to suffer two shocks in one morning.

**Mrs Macdonald** Yes. (*It sinks in*) Eh? How d'you mean? Two shocks?

**Mr Meany** (*dropping his oily leer*) Go on, Sergeant. Get on with it.

**Sergeant Sweet** (*uncomfortable*) Right, sir. Now, you be Mrs A.M.J.J.A. Macdonald. Right?

**Mrs Macdonald** Right.

**Sergeant Sweet** You be living on this farm. Right?

**Mrs Macdonald** Right.

**Sergeant Sweet** The farm belongs to Mr Meany. Right?

**Mrs Macdonald** Right.

**Sergeant Sweet** You pays rent to Mr Meany. Right?

**Mrs Macdonald** Right.

**Mr Meany** Wrong. She hasn't paid the rent for weeks. It's a disgrace.

**Jack** It *is* a disgrace. Mr Meany puts his rents up and up and up, so however hard Mum works she can never make enough money to pay him.

*The animals all voice their agreement*

**Mr Meany** Slander! You heard that, Sergeant. Arrest that boy.

**Jack** *He* should be arrested. Mum has to sell him all the farm produce and he pays her a measly rotten price. Why else do you think we have to have parties of paying visitors?

*He indicates the audience. Sergeant Sweet and Mr Meany "see" the audience*

**Mrs Macdonald** (*to the audience*) Nothing personal, you understand. You're very welcome!

**Mr Meany** (*exploding*) Visitors? They're trespassing! On my land! Arrest them *all*, Sergeant. Lock them up.

**Sergeant Sweet** Hang on, sir.

**Mr Meany** I will not hang on. I demand action. Arrest those trespassers!

*Jack steps forward*

**Jack** Go away. Scram! Or I'll——

**Mr Meany** Ooh! Threats! You heard that, Sergeant. Where are your handcuffs? (*He grabs Jack*)

**Mrs Macdonald** Take your hands off my son.

### Music 2D: Underscore

*She grabs Jack, and she and Mr Meany pull him back and forth. Everyone starts shouting. The animals make protesting noises*

| **Jack** | | | Let me go! . . . *etc.* |
|---|---|---|---|
| **Mr Meany** | | | I'll teach you . . . *etc.* |
| **Mrs Macdonald** | (*together*) | | Let him go! . . . *etc.* |
| **Sergeant Sweet** | | | Break it up . . . *etc.* |

*Pandemonium*

*Dog enters, sees what is happening, and rushes up to Mr Meany and bites his leg*

*Mr Meany lets go of Jack, turns and aims a kick at Dog*

**Mr Meany** Arrest that animal, Sergeant. It bit me.

*The animals moo and boo him. Pandemonium again*

*Jeannie enters*

**Jeannie** What on earth's going on?

*Everyone stops and turns to her*

**Mrs Macdonald** It's Mr Meany, Jeannie. He wants his rent.

**Mr Meany** I want more than that. I want them *out*. Now. Sergeant, do your duty. Throw them out. Lock them up.

**Sergeant Sweet** (*taking control*) That won't be necessary, sir, not yet anyway. Mrs Macdonald, have you the money to pay Mr Meany his rent?

**Mrs Macdonald** No, Sergeant. (*She has an idea*) Unless he'd accept our barley harvest instead—Jeannie's been out mowing the meadow.

**Jeannie** It's no good, Mum. All that rain last week's rotted the barley. It's worthless.

**Mr Meany** There you are. They're refusing to pay. Lock them up.

**Sergeant Sweet** No, sir. That's not fair. They're not refusing to pay. They've got no money. That be very different. According to my rule book——

*He refers to it. The animals peep over his shoulder*

—Mrs Macdonald has twenty-four hours to find the money and give it to Mr Meany. Or else, I'm sorry to say, madam, you and your family and your animals will have to leave. All right?

**Mrs Macdonald** Thank you, Sergeant.

**Sergeant Sweet** All right, sir?

**Mr Meany** No, it's all wrong. They should be forced to go *now*. Still, (*with a leer*) I suppose this gives you time to pack, dear lady.

*Rumblings from the animals*

**Sergeant Sweet** I'll see you both same time, same place tomorrow.

*He exits*

*The animals turn towards Mr Meany*

**Mr Meany** Well. I'll bid you good-day.

**Mrs Macdonald** As you said, Mr Meany, a good day for *you*.

**Jack** And a rotten one for us. Thanks to you.

**Mrs Macdonald** Jack . . .

**Mr Meany** Don't take that tone with me, young man . . .

### Music 2E: Tension Music

*The animals, led by Dog, close in on him, leading him to the feeding trough downstage. They start mooing and booing*

(*Nervous*) Let me pass. Stand back.

*They edge him further forward*

It's not my fault you're in this mess . . .

*Plop. He falls in the trough and is covered from head to foot with "pig swill". Hopefully he gets up and out of the trough, spluttering with rage*

**Jack** (*imitating Mr Meany*) It's not our fault you're in this mess!

*Laughter*

**Mr Meany** You'll pay, you'll see. You'll be locked up, the lot of you!

*He exits. If it is impracticable for him to exit covered with "pig swill", he should be wheeled out in the trough by Jack and Jeannie*

*The laughter and booing die. All become very quiet and serious*

### Music 2F: Wistful Music

*All gather round Mrs Macdonald, who embraces them, sitting in their midst like a mother hen. Eventually . . .*

**Jack** What are we going to do, Mum?

**Mrs Macdonald** Well, dearie, we'll never get the money by tomorrow. And Mr Meany means business.

**Jeannie** (*having an idea*) We could sell something.

**Mrs Macdonald** Sell what, dearie?
**Jeannie** Well ... (*She looks around. Reluctantly*) Pig?

*Pig protectively embraces the Piglets*

**Mrs Macdonald** Oh no, dearie. Pig's got piglets to look after.
**Jack** Duck?

*Duck protectively embraces the Ducklings*

**Mrs Macdonald** No, dearie. Duck's got ducklings to look after.
**Jeannie** (*uncertainly*) Dog?

*Dog hugs Jack for protection*

**Jack** No, Jeannie, he's our pet.
**Mrs Macdonald** It's true. He's one of the family, really, aren't you, Dog?

*Dog comes and nuzzles up against her*

**Jeannie** That only leaves ... Marigold.

*The music stops. Marigold looks sadly from side to side and moos gently*

**Mrs Macdonald** (*reluctantly*) You're right, dearie. (*She goes to Marigold, and puts her arm round her*) I'm sorry, Marigold. It's the only way. We don't want to see you go, but ... well, you did play me up rotten when I tried to milk you and ... as soon as we can, we'll buy you back. (*She calls*) Jack.
**Jack** Yes, Mum?
**Mrs Macdonald** Take her to market and get the best price you can.
**Jack** Yes, Mum.

*Dog pulls Jack's sleeve, indicating he wants to go too*

Can Dog come too? Marigold was his special friend.
**Mrs Macdonald** Of course he can.

### Song 3: Marigold

*During the song, Marigold goes round to all the animals, bidding them farewell. As they sing, Jack and Dog lead her off, possibly through the auditorium*

| (*Singing*) | Marigold, Marigold<br>Sad to say, must be sold<br>Marigold, Marigold<br>Sad to see you go. |
|---|---|
| **Mrs Macdonald,**<br>**Jeannie,**<br>**Jack, (Dog),**<br>**Pigs, Ducks** | Marigold, Marigold<br>Sad to say, must be sold<br>Marigold, Marigold<br>Sad to say goodbye. |

So faithful friend farewell, you

Know we don't want to sell you
But what else is left
For us to do?
We will miss your milk
We will miss your moo
But most of all
We'll miss you.

Marigold, Marigold
Sad to say, must be sold
Marigold, Marigold
Sad to see you go.

Marigold, Marigold
Sad to say, must be sold
Marigold, Marigold
Sad to say goodbye
**Mrs Macdonald**    Sad to say goodbye.

*Marigold, Jack and Dog have gone*

(*Speaking, seeing how sad everyone is*) Right. Peckers up, everybody. Back
to work. (*To the Pigs*) Back to the sty. (*To the Ducks*) Back to the pond.
(*To Jeannie*) Back to the grindstone. Let's go and clean out the cowshed
... (*Realizing*) Not that we need to now, really ... (*She is tearful*)
**Jeannie** Let's do it anyway, Mum.

### Music 3A: Exit Music

*All exit various ways, leaving the stage empty*

*Pause. A sudden lighting effect tells us something odd is about to happen. An
electronic roaring noise*

*A spaceship enters and lands. If possible it flies in from above, smoke
belching forth from its tail, and lights flashing. The spaceship could be a
cut-out, with a practical door or hatch. Access could be through a
stage-trap, or from the wings, if the spaceship is adjacent to them. The door
or hatch opens, accompanied by a whirring noise*

*Beep, a spaceman, enters, walking rather mechanically. He should be
coloured predominantly silver, and if possible have a flashing light and/or
moving parts, such as a revolving antenna. On his back is his
name--"Beep", and various controls, knobs, etc., should be incorporated
into his costume. (*NB: *The "Buzz" and "Beep" noises can be either spoken
or electronic*)

**Beep** (*as he emerges*) *Beep. Beep. Beep. Beep. Beep.* (*He looks around as if to
check for safety. Then he takes a small battery pack walkie-talkie and
speaks into it; this could be attached to his costume, or on a curly coloured
wire*) Beep to Buzz. Beep to Buzz. All clear. *Beep.* All clear. *Beep.*
Dis—em—bark. *Beep.* Dis—em—bark.

*From the spaceship, Buzz enters. He should look similar to Beep, but be a different shape. For example, if Beep is tall and thin, Buzz should be short and round. He too has lights, antenna etc., and "Buzz" on his back, plus various controls. He should look funnier than Beep if possible. He carries a silver suitcase or hold-all*

**Buzz** (*a buzzing noise*) *Buzz. Buzz. Buzz. Buzz. Buzz. (He stops and stands looking vacantly out front. He continues to jerk, as though his "engine" is still running. His head nods up and down) Buzz. Buzz. Buzz. Buzz.*

**Beep** *Beep.* Ready to explore?

**Buzz** *Buzz. Buzz. Buzz.*

**Beep** *Beep.* North or south? North or south?

**Buzz** *Buzz. Buzz. Buzz.*

**Beep** Beep to Buzz. Are—you—A—one—O—K?

*He approaches Buzz, who continues his jerky movement*

**Buzz** *Buzz. Buzz. Buzz. (Suddenly he drops the suitcase on Beep's foot)*

**Beep** Ow. You clumsy *beep, beep, beep, beep, beep. (He punches Buzz, hitting one of his controls)*

*Buzz comes out with a stream of gobbledegook. This is accompanied by even more jerky, quirky movements, including the odd arm shooting out which makes Beep duck. After a couple of these, Beep ducks but Buzz changes the rhythm so that Beep gets hit as he straightens up*

**Beep** Ow! (*He manages to press a control on Buzz's back*) Aut—o—mat—ic cut—out!

*Buzz stops still in a frozen position*

Do you receive me? *Beep.* Buzz, do you receive me?

**Buzz** (*as though in a trance*) *Buzz.*

**Beep** You are suffering from space hiccups. Stand by for tuning. *Beep.* Stand by for tuning. (*Beep twiddles a tuning knob*)

---

## OPTIONAL

*As he twiddles we hear electronic noises, interference, etc., as though he were tuning in to a radio. Snatches of "The Archers" signature tune, perhaps, or the news "Pips", with which Beep might try to have a conversation ... these sounds, though familiar to the audience, are alien to Beep*

---

*Eventually ...*

**Buzz** (*varying between high and low frequency*) *Bzzzzzzzzzzzzz.*

*Beep twiddles knob till the buzz is constant*

**Beep** *Beep.* Testing, testing. (*He presses a button*)

**Buzz** (*very deep low voice*) One. Two. Buckle my shoe. Three, four ...

**Beep** Cancel. *Beep.* Cancel. (*He presses the button*) *Beep.* Testing, testing.

**Buzz** (*a very high voice*) One, two, buckle my shoe, three, four knock at the door, five, six——

*Beep deliberately turns the knob gradually*

> (*Slowing and voice lowering*) —pick up sticks, seven, eight, shut the gate, nine, ten, start again, one, two, buckle my shoe, three, four, knock at the door . . . (*the voice goes lower and slower than "normal", then starts to rise again*) . . . five, six, pick up sticks, seven, eight, shut the gate——

*Beep "sets" Buzz's tone*

> —shut the gate, shut the gate, shut the gate . . .

*Beep presses the control on Buzz's back*

**Beep** Aut—o—mat—ic cut—out!

*Buzz freezes*

> Are you A—one—O—K now? *Beep.* Feeling better? (*He switches Buzz on*)

**Buzz** (*staccato*) Much—I—now—better—thank—feel—you—sticks—three —knock—my—seven—buckle—pick—eight—gate—again—two—four —ten—shut—up—the—the—on—six—five—one—shoe—start—nine —much—I—now—better—thank—feel—you——

*During this, Beep realizes things are not right and opens the suitcase, takes out a silver screwdriver and oilcan. He pours oil down Buzz's throat*

> —glug—glug—glug—glug—much—thank—feel—I—now—you— thank—better——

*Beep tweaks with the screwdriver. Buzz eventually "gets better"*

> —feel—better—feel—thank—now—you—much—better—feel—now— I—thank—you—I—feel—much—better—now—I—feel—much— better—now—thank—you. (*He stops—normal again*)

**Beep** Good. *Beep.* Ready to explore?

**Buzz** *Buzz.* Ready to explore. (*He picks up the suitcase*)

---

### OPTIONAL

**Beep** *Beep.* Scanner probe on?

**Buzz** *Buzz.* Scanner probe on.

*They turn on lamps in their helmets—like miners' lamps. Perhaps an electronic noise accompanies the light. They make their lights shine on the audience*

---

*They walk forward*

**Beep** ⎱ (*together*) ⎰ *Beep. Beep. Beep. Beep.*
**Buzz** ⎰           ⎱ *Buzz. Buzz. Buzz. Buzz.*

*Suddenly Buzz sees the audience. He stops*

**Buzz** (*short sharp buzzes*) *Bzz. Bzz. Bzz. Bzz.*
**Beep** *Beep.* What?
**Buzz** *Buzz.* Beings, Beep. Beings.
**Beep** *Beep.* Checking. Checking. (*He looks at or shines his light on individuals*) Affirmative. Affirmative. *Beep.* Beings, Buzz, beings.
**Buzz** *Buzz.* Are they friendly? *Buzz.* They look friendly.
**Beep** Checking for friendliness. (*To the audience, as though saying "Hallo"*) *Beep beep.*
**Audience** *Beep beep.*
**Beep** *Beep, beep, beep.*
**Audience** *Beep, beep, beep.*
**Buzz** *Buzz, buzz.*
**Audience** *Buzz, buzz.*
**Buzz** *Buzz, buzz, buzz.*
**Audience** *Buzz, buzz, buzz.*
**Beep** Affirmative. Friendly beings. *Beep.* Let us communicate.

### Song 4: Beep! Buzz!

**Beep & Buzz**      Greetings earthlings, let us teach
                     You to speak some spaceman speech

*They encourage the audience to join in, repeating each word/sound. If required, Beep and Buzz could divide the words/sounds between them*

| | |
|---|---|
| **Beep** | Beep |
| **Audience** | Beep |
| **Buzz** | Buzz |
| **Audience** | Buzz |
| **Beep & Buzz** | Plop |
| **Audience** | Plop |
| **Beep & Buzz** | Boing |
| **Audience** | Boing |
| **Beep & Buzz** | Vroom |
| **Audience** | Vroom |
| **Beep & Buzz** | Ping |
| **Audience** | Ping |
| **Beep & Buzz** | SSSSSS |
| **Audience** | SSSSSS |
| **Beep & Buzz** | Gedoing |
| **Audience** | Gedoing |

**Beep & Buzz**      Friendly earthlings we are sure
                     You would like to learn some more.

                     Brrrrr
**Audience**         Brrrrr
**Beep & Buzz**      Plink

| | |
|---|---|
| **Audience** | Plink |
| **Beep & Buzz** | Clicketty-clack |
| **Audience** | Clicketty-clack |
| **Beep & Buzz** | Honk |
| **Audience** | Honk |
| **Beep & Buzz** | Squeak |
| **Audience** | Squeak |
| **Beep & Buzz** | Pow |
| **Audience** | Pow |
| **Beep & Buzz** | Wheeeee |
| **Audience** | Wheeeee |
| **Beep & Buzz** | Kerplonk |
| **Audience** | Kerplonk |
| | |
| **Beep & Buzz** | Now our lingo you all know |
| | So let's have another go. |
| | |
| **Beep** | Beep |
| **Audience** | Beep |
| **Buzz** | Buzz |
| **Audience** | Buzz |
| **Beep & Buzz** | Plop |
| **Audience** | Plop |
| **Beep & Buzz** | Boing |
| **Audience** | Boing |
| **Beep & Buzz** | Vroom |
| **Audience** | Vroom |
| **Beep & Buzz** | Ping |
| **Audience** | Ping |
| **Beep & Buzz** | SSSSSS |
| **Audience** | SSSSSS |
| **Beep & Buzz** | Gedoing |
| **Audience** | Gedoing |
| | |
| **Beep & Buzz** | Brrrrr |
| **Audience** | Brrrrr |
| **Beep & Buzz** | Plink |
| **Audience** | Plink |
| **Beep & Buzz** | Clicketty-clack |
| **Audience** | Clicketty-clack |
| **Beep & Buzz** | Honk |
| **Audience** | Honk |
| **Beep & Buzz** | Squeak |
| **Audience** | Squeak |
| **Beep & Buzz** | Pow |
| **Audience** | Pow |
| **Beep & Buzz** | Wheeeee |
| **Audience** | Wheeeee |

**Beep & Buzz**      Kerplonk
**Audience**          Kerplonk.

*Beep and Buzz applaud the audience*

*After the song, Buzz takes out a silver book entitled "The Universe A–Z".*

**Beep** (*to the audience*) Please. *Beep*. Friendly beings, help us.
**Buzz** *Buzz*. Is this the Milky Way?
**Audience** No.
**Beep** *Beep*. This is not the Milky Way?
**Audience** No.
**Buzz** *Buzz*. Then where are we?
**Audience** (*there may be several answers*) Mrs Macdonald's farmyard/*local town*/Earth/England.
**Beep** *Beep*. Mrs Macdonald's Farmyard/*local town*/Earth/England?
**Audience** Yes.
**Buzz** (*checking his A–Z*) *Buzz*. But Mrs Macdonald's Farmyard/*local town*/Earth/England is nowhere near the Milky Way. *Buzz*. We wanted to reach the Milky Way because we wanted some "milk". *Buzz*. Repeat. "Milk".
**Beep** *Beep*. Do you know what "milk" is?
**Audience** Yes.
**Beep** *Beep*. From where does it come?
**Audience** Cows.
**Beep** *Beep*. Where?
**Audience** Cows.
**Beep** *Beep*. (*To Buzz*) Cows.

*Buzz has been checking in his A–Z*

**Buzz** (*excited*) Small town on Isle of Wight. *Buzz* (*To the audience*) Right?
**Audience** No.
**Beep** *Beep*. What cows then?
**Audience** Animals/moo-cows.
**Buzz** Aha! *Buzz*. (*He returns to the suitcase and brings out another large book of animal pictures—or a set of cards with animal pictures. He holds up a picture of a giraffe*)
**Beep** *Beep*. Cow?
**Audience** No.

*Buzz holds up a picture of a monkey*

**Buzz** *Buzz*. Cow?
**Audience** No.

*Buzz holds up a picture of a tortoise*

**Buzz** *Buzz*. Cow?
**Audience** No.

*Buzz holds up a picture of a cow*

**Buzz** *Buzz*. Cow?

**Audience** Yes.

*Beep leaps forward*

**Beep** *Beep.* Cow?
**Audience** Yes.
**Beep** *Beep.* (*Doubtful*) Milk comes from *this*?
**Audience** Yes.
**Buzz** *Buzz.* What noise does cow make?
**Audience** Moo.

*Buzz and Beep react surprised*

**Buzz** *Buzz.* Moo?
**Audience** Yes.
**Beep** Sounds highly unlikely. *Beep.* Friendly beings are joking with us. Ho ho ho. Yes?
**Audience** No.
**Beep** (*with a shrug*) Very well. *Beep.* For milk we need cow. Friendly beings. Thank you. (*He bows*)
**Buzz** *Buzz.* Thank you. (*He bows*)

### Song 4A: Beep! Buzz! (Reprise)

| | |
|---|---|
| **Beep & Buzz** | Earthlings we must hurry now |
| | Off on Operation Cow. |
| **Beep** | Beep |
| **Audience** | Beep |
| **Buzz** | Buzz |
| **Audience** | Buzz |
| **Beep & Buzz** | Bye! |
| **Audience** | Bye! |

*They exit*


SCENE 2

*On the Road*

*This could be a frontcloth scene. There is a signpost pointing to the market (1 mile) in one direction and Mrs Macdonald's farm (4 miles) in the other*

### Music 4B: Entrance Music

*Jack, Marigold and Dog enter, possibly through the auditorium. Jack and Marigold are tired, having been on the road some time; Dog still has plenty of bounce*

**Jack** (*limping to a halt*) We've walked miles. My feet are like lumps of lead. How are your hooves, Marigold? Heavy?

*Marigold moos and mimes that her hooves are indeed heavy. Dog barks and points to the signpost*

What? Another mile to go?

*Dog barks, and sets off towards the market*

Hang on. Tell you what. Let's have a rest before we go on, eh?

*Marigold moos gratefully and sinks to her knees. Dog shrugs in agreement and returns*

That's it Marigold. Get a bit of cow kip.

*Jack lies on the ground. Marigold moos "good-night"*

Night!

*Dog starts to settle too. Marigold snores. Jack suddenly sits up with a jump*

Hey! (*He lowers his voice and whispers to Dog, glancing occasionally at Marigold, who continues to snore gently*) We'd better not go to sleep, just in case Marigold wanders off. I mean, you couldn't really blame her if she tried to escape. *I* would if someone wanted to sell me.

*Dog nods, then mimes and woofs that Jack should sleep; he—Dog—will stay awake*

What? Me go to sleep? You stay awake? Are you sure?

*Dog barks, and bounces energetically*

You're not tired at all?

*Dog barks*

All right then. Thanks. (*Firmly*) But don't drop off!

*Dog barks, offended. Jack settles to sleep. Dog watches. Suddenly Jack sits up*

Are you sure you won't fall asleep?

*Dog barks in Jack's face, making him jump. Jack settles to sleep. Dog watches. Suddenly Jack sits up again*

You're not dropping off, are you?

*Dog barks in Jack's face, making him jump. Jack settles to sleep. Dog watches. Suddenly Jack sits up again. Before he can say a word, Dog barks in his face. Jack jumps, then, reassured, settles to sleep*

**Music 4C: Incidental Music**

*Dog goes into a short comedy "falling to sleep" routine. His eyes start shutting involuntarily, his head droops; then suddenly he wakes up and is cross with himself. His eyes close again. Head droops. Sudden wake-up. Cross with himself. The third time his body droops too, and sinks to the ground. Again he wakes, and bounces about to keep awake. Finally he sinks gently to sleep, snoring loudly. The audience have hopefully been shouting to Dog to keep awake*

*After a pause, tension music (4C continued) as Beep and Buzz enter, carrying their cow picture. Seeing the sleeping group, they advance gingerly towards them*

*(NB: The audience may well be torn in their loyalties, because they "like" both sets of characters, but their main concern should be to wake up Jack, Dog and Marigold, in order to avoid the kidnap of Marigold. So, hopefully, the audience will be shouting out during this sequence)*

*Beep and Buzz look at Dog and check him against the picture. They shake their heads and pass on to Jack. They check him against the picture, then shake their heads. Finally they come to Marigold. They check her against the picture and get very excited. (If necessary, though audience noise will probably render it redundant, Marigold could suddenly "moo" as part of her snoring—this would confirm to Beep and Buzz that she is a cow). They mime that she is too big to lift. Beep has an idea, and whispers to Buzz*

*Buzz registers this as a good idea and speeds off, returning immediately with a silver space vacuum cleaner*

*This could be a cylindrical container on casters, complete with flashing lights, etc. A thick, flexible hose or tube leads from it, and has attached to it a funnel-shaped nozzle. It makes a loud vacuum-sucking noise. (If necessary, just the nozzle and tube would suffice.)*

*Beep and Buzz advance on Marigold, who wakes up, and is sucked backwards towards the nozzle. By now the audience should be shouting out, but Jack and Dog remain asleep. Marigold manages to force herself free and runs away. A short chase, at the end of which the vacuum power is re-established. Marigold is dragged backwards. Suddenly Jack wakes up, sees what is happening, and wakes up Dog. They both grab Marigold's front end and pull her against the vacuum suction*

*A few seconds of stale-mate tug-of-war, in which both spacemen are heaving on the nozzle and Jack and Dog are heaving on Marigold. Dog suddenly has an idea, and nips round to the cylinder of the vacuum cleaner, finds the lever marked ON/OFF, and turns it off. Spacemen and Jack, the vacuum suction having been turned off, fall over. Marigold remains standing c.*
*(NB: In the original production, the vacuum idea was omitted and Beep and Buzz simply pulled Marigold's tail. This worked, but the vacuum idea might be more fun) Dog rushes to the spacemen, barking. The spacemen react terrified*

**Beep** } *(together)* { *Beep! Beep! Beep! Beep!*
**Buzz** } { *Buzz! Buzz! Buzz! Buzz!*
**Jack** *(getting up)* What's going on? What do you think you're up to? Dog—leave.

*Dog returns to Jack, leaving Beep and Buzz on the ground*

Who are you, anyway?
**Beep** *Beep.* I am Beep.
**Buzz** *Buzz.* I am Buzz.

**Beep** Apologies, friendly being. *Beep.* We will return to our spaceship directly.

**Buzz** (*gathering up the vacuum machine*) Forgive us, friendly being. *Buzz.* Forgive us.

**Jack** Hang on. Spaceship? Did you say spaceship?

**Beep** Affirmative. I said spaceship. *Beep.* How else do you think we came here?

**Jack** Where is it? Could I see it?

**Beep** *Beep.* (*Suspicious*) Why?

**Jack** (*a bit embarrassed*) Because I er . . . well . . . I've been building a sort of spaceship—a rocket; just as a sort of hobby thing. I'd really like to see a real one.

*Beep and Buzz look at each other and nod*

**Beep** See. *Beep.* Over there. (*He points off-stage*)

**Jack** (*with a gasp*) Gosh. It's fantastic.

**Buzz** *Buzz.* Like your rocket?

**Jack** Hardly. Well, I mean . . . actually my rocket's got a slight technical hitch . . . quite a big technical hitch actually . . . it er . . . it won't start.

**Beep** *Beep.* You need extra boosters.

**Buzz** *Buzz.* (*Nodding*) Extra boosters.

**Jack** Really?

*Marigold moos*

**Buzz** Moo! We were right. *Buzz.* This *is* a cow.

**Jack** Yes, it is. *My* cow. What were *you* doing trying to hijack her?

**Beep** *Beep.* Apologies, friendly being. We did not know the cow was yours. *Beep.* We badly need a cow. For our master . . .

**Buzz** *Buzz.* The Silver Giant.

**Jack** The Silver Giant?

**Beep** Affirmative. *Beep.* But if the cow is yours . . .

**Buzz** We bid you farewell. *Buzz.*

**Beep** *Beep.*

*They start to go*

**Jack** Wait. Suppose I said that Marigold—the cow—was for sale. What would you give me for her?

**Beep** Conference. *Beep.*

*Beep and Buzz huddle for a tête-à-tête*

**Buzz** ⎫ (*whispering together*) ⎰ *Buzz, Buzz, Buzz, Buzz.*
**Beep** ⎭                            ⎱ *Beep, Beep, Beep, Beep.*

*Eventually . . .*

**Beep** *Beep.* In exchange for the cow we will give you extra boosters for your rocket.

**Jack** (*excited*) Really?

*Dog barks, as if to say "Don't accept"*

What? Don't do it? But if I had those extra boosters, I could get my rocket working.

**Beep** *Beep.* Take it.

**Buzz** *Buzz.* Or leave it.

**Jack** (*to the audience*) What do you think I should do? Take it? Or leave it?

*The audience shout out advice. Jack makes his decision, even if he has to go against the audience's advice*

(*To Beep and Buzz*) I'll take it. Thank you.

### Music 4D: Incidental Music

*The spacemen, taking the space vacuum cleaner with them, show Jack towards the spaceship. Jack leads Marigold. Dog follows. They all exit (or walk through the auditorium) as the set changes back to reveal Mrs Macdonald's Farmyard of Scene 1*


SCENE 3

*Mrs Macdonald's Farmyard*

*The spaceship stands in all its glory*

*All enter (or return to the stage)*

*Jack reacts excitedly to the spaceship. Beep replaces the space vacuum cleaner, and Buzz brings out half a dozen silver cylinders, which look like label-less tins of food (which is exactly what they are). Jack receives them with awed thanks and puts them in his pockets. He hands over Marigold to Beep and Buzz. Jack and Dog wave as Marigold is taken on board the spaceship. Beep and Buzz wave farewell. The hatch/door is closed. Jack and Dog watch as the spaceship starts up*

*Smoke. Flashing lights. Then it takes off and disappears*

*All goes quiet. Dog whines. Jack hugs him*

**Jack** Sorry, Dog. I know Marigold was your special friend.

*Dog nods and whines more*

### Song 5: Keep Your Pecker Up

(*Singing*)    If saying goodbye
            Makes your nose go dry
            And your tail start sagging
            Instead of wagging—
            Just listen to me
            And maybe you'll see
            Though she's gone

Life goes on
If you try
You'll get by.

You gotta
Keep your pecker up
Keep your pecker up
When you feel upset
It's a fair old bet
If you put a brave face on
You'll forget
You can do it if you just try
To keep your pecker held high.

Keep your pecker up
Keep your pecker up
Keep your pecker up
High high high
Keep your pecker up
Keep your pecker up
Keep a check that you
Keep your pecker up
High.

*The music continues*

*Duck and Ducklings, plus Pig and Piglets, enter*

(*Speaking*)  Hallo ducks! Hallo pigs.

*All look depressed*

What's the matter? Are you missing Marigold too?

*They nod*

Then listen . . .

(*Singing*)        You gotta
Keep your pecker up
Keep your pecker up
Never sit and mope
Never give up hope
If you make a big effort
You can cope
It's as easy as apple pie
Just keep your pecker held high.

Keep your pecker up
Keep your pecker up
Keep your pecker up
High high high

Keep your pecker up
Keep your pecker up
Keep a check that you
Keep your pecker up
High.

*The Ducks and Pigs join in. All grow happier*

**All**                You gotta
Keep your pecker up
Keep your pecker up
Keep your pecker up
High high high
Keep your pecker up
Keep your pecker up
Keep a check that you
Keep your pecker up
High.

*Towards the end of the song, Mrs Macdonald and Jeannie enter. Perhaps they join in the final chorus*

You gotta
Keep your pecker up
Keep your pecker up
Keep your pecker up
High high high
Keep your pecker up
Keep your pecker up
Keep a check that you
Keep your pecker up
Keep your pecker up
Keep your pecker up
Keep a check that you
Keep your pecker up
High.

High!

**Mrs Macdonald** Welcome back, Jack Mac. How did you get on?
**Jeannie** Did you sell Marigold?
**Mrs Macdonald** Of course he did, dearie. Didn't you, Jack?
**Jack** Yes, Mum.
**Mrs Macdonald** Good lad.
**Jeannie** We can stay here after all?
**Mrs Macdonald** Of course we can, dearie. Can't we, Jack?
**Jack** Well ...
**Jeannie** Have you got the money?
**Mrs Macdonald** Of course he has. Haven't you, Jack?

*Pause*

Haven't you, Jack?

*Pause*

*Haven't you, Jack?*

**Jack** In a manner of speaking, Mum.

**Mrs Macdonald** What manner of speaking? I only know one manner of speaking. *Plain* speaking. So let's have it. What did you get for Marigold?

**Jack** (*taking the boosters out*) These, Mum.

*The animals all crowd round to look*

**Mrs Macdonald** What are they?

**Jack** Extra boosters, Mum.

**Mrs Macdonald** Extra what?

**Jack** Boosters ... for my rocket.

**Jeannie** Oh, Jack ...

*She takes one, and runs indoors, in tears*

**Mrs Macdonald** I could scream ... I'm *going* to scream ... Aaaaaaaaaaaaah!

*She advances on Jack, who retreats*

Your head isn't in the clouds, my lad. Your head's in the ground. It's a great fat turnip.

**Jack** I'm sorry, Mum. I thought ...

**Mrs Macdonald** That's just it. You didn't think. You never think. You're thoughtless. (*Starting to cry*) Jeannie and I work our fingers to the bone while you just fiddle around with your silly rocket. And now what's to become of us? We can't pay Mr Meany. We've lost our home. We've lost Marigold ... where is poor Marigold, anyway?

**Jack** With Beep and Buzz.

**Mrs Macdonald** Beep and Buzz?

**Jack** The spacemen.

**Mrs Macdonald** Spacemen? (*She cannot believe her ears*) Spacemen? Jack, do you think you ought to lie down?

**Jack** No, Mum. Spacemen who work for the Silver Giant.

**Mrs Macdonald** 'Cos either you're round the twist or I am. Silver Giant? Spacemen?

**Jack** They came down in a spaceship.

**Mrs Macdonald** Spaceship? There was never a spaceship. (*To the audience*) Was there?

**Audience** Yes.

*Jack and Dog join in*

**Mrs Macdonald** Oh no there wasn't.

**Audience** Oh yes there was.

**Mrs Macdonald** Oh no there wasn't.

**Audience** Oh yes there was.

**Mrs Macdonald** Maybe *you* ought to lie down, too!

*Jeannie runs out of the farmhouse carrying the booster, and a plate*

**Jeannie** Mum. I've opened one of Jack's boosters.
**Jack** Oh, Jeannie, you've ruined it.
**Jeannie** (*gently*) I don't think so, Jack.
**Mrs Macdonald** Why, what's inside?
**Jeannie** (*after a pause*) Baked beans.

*She tips some out on to the plate. Stunned pause*

**Jack** (*appalled*) Baked beans?
**Jeannie** They took the labels off the tins.
**Mrs Macdonald** You sold Marigold for six tins of label-less baked beans?
**Jack** But . . .
**Mrs Macdonald** (*grabbing a broom and attacking Jack*) Why didn't you sell Dog for a packet of fish fingers while you were at it? Then you could sell me—I might be worth half a pound of sausages.
**Jack** But . . .
**Mrs Macdonald** Go to bed before I bash your brains out. Not that you've *got* any brains to bash out.

*The animals scatter as Jack dashes into the farmhouse*

(*To Dog*) And you go to your kennel. I might have expected this from Jack, but not you. Selling your best friend for a saucy snack.

*Dog sadly retreats to his kennel. The Pigs and Ducks look on, nervously*

What are you lot gawping at? Go on. Hop it. (*Pointing*) Sty. Pond.

*The animals exit*

*Mrs Macdonald is left with Jeannie. Pause*

**Jeannie** (*quietly*) Jack didn't mean it, Mum.
**Mrs Macdonald** I know, dearie. (*She sighs*) But Mr Meany means it, Jeannie.

*Jeannie nods. Pause*

**Jeannie** Night, Mum.
**Mrs Macdonald** Night, dearie.

*Jeannie goes inside, taking the baked beans*

*Mrs Macdonald starts to go in, then turns back to the audience*

There never was a spaceship. Was there?
**Audience** Yes.
**Mrs Macdonald** No.
**Audience** Yes.
**Mrs Macdonald** (*staggered*) Just checking . . .

### Music 5A: Scene Change

*She goes inside, shaking her head in disbelief*

*The Lighting changes as the farmhouse starts to revolve, or as the frontage is removed to reveal the interior*

Scene 4

*Inside the Farmhouse*

*The only necessary practical area is a bedroom, shared by all three Mac-donalds. Ideally this would be on the first floor, reached by a winding staircase. If so, the room below would best be a kitchen/living area. Jack and Jeannie are already in their beds, ostensibly asleep. Cosy candlelight effect*

*Mrs Macdonald enters through the front door and wearily climbs the stairs. She arrives in the bedroom, checks that Jack and Jeannie are asleep, then goes into a comedy undressing scene*

**Music 5B: Incidental Music**

*This should not be a cod striptease done to raunchy music, but an amusing string of surprises as garments are removed to reveal unlikely undergarments. Perhaps she has masses of skirts, or never-ending stockings. Needless to say, her nightie is the final layer. Perhaps her hat, when removed, reveals a hairnet and rollers. If required, the routine could be extended to include the putting on of a creamy facepack or the cleaning of teeth, depending on the director and actor playing Mrs Macdonald. The routine should not take over the play, however!*

*When she is ready for bed, Mrs Macdonald pulls down the bedclothes, then leaps into bed in one deft movement. Immediately she leaps high and out of bed again*

**Mrs Macdonald** Aaaaaaaaaah!

*Jack and Jeannie wake up*

**Jeannie** What's up?

*Mrs Macdonald investigates, and finds, in her bed, the baked bean tin boosters*

**Mrs Macdonald** I've got baked beans in my bed, that's what's up. I nearly took off.
**Jack** Maybe they *are* extra boosters after all. (*He laughs*)
**Mrs Macdonald** Jack.
**Jack** Sorry Mum.
**Mrs Macdonald** (*picking up the tins*) Wretched things. (*She opens the window and starts throwing them out. One. Two.* NB: *If possible the lighting should isolate the farmhouse so that we don't see exactly where the tins fall*) Done enough damage.

*Throw. Thud. A howl from the kennel area*

(*Calling*) Sorry, Dog.

*Throw*

Not having them in the house a second longer.

*Throw (the last one)*

Has-beans! (*She gets into bed*) Nightie-night.

**Jack**
**Jeannie** } (*together*) { Night Mum.

*All settle to sleep*

---

## OPTIONAL

*Mrs Macdonald blows out her candle, and settles. After four or five seconds the candle relights. The audience wake up Mrs Macdonald to tell her. She thanks them, blows it out again, then settles again. Pause. Again the candle relights itself. The audience shout out. Mrs Macdonald thanks them, blows it out again, then settles. The same thing again. As a pay-off, Jack's candle now relights itself; the audience shout. Mrs Macdonald cannot see Jack's candle, and accuses the audience of having her on. Finally, unseen by Mrs Macdonald, Jack wakes up and blows out his candle, just as Mrs Macdonald turns to see it. Still thinking the audience were teasing, she settles again*

---

*Pause. A snore or two from Mrs Macdonald. Suddenly a little voice ...*

**Jack** Mum.
**Mrs Macdonald** Mm ... (*She turns over, trying not to hear*)
**Jack** (*after a pause*) Mum.
**Mrs Macdonald** Yes?
**Jack** I can't sleep.
**Mrs Macdonald** Snap. Neither can I.
**Jack** Why not?
**Mrs Macdonald** My horrible little boy keeps waking me up. Go to sleep.
**Jack** Yes, Mum.

*Pause they settle*

Mum.

*Mrs Macdonald grunts and turns over*

(*After a pause*) Mum.
**Mrs Macdonald** Yes?
**Jack** I still can't sleep.

*Mrs Macdonald growls through her teeth*

I can't stop thinking about Marigold, Mum. And the baked beans. I'm sorry I was so stupid. I really am.

*Mrs Macdonald gets out of bed and sits with Jack*

**Mrs Macdonald** Something'll turn up, dearie. You'll see. Come on, close your eyes.

## Song 6: Sweet Dreams

(*Singing*)              The moon his watch is keeping
                         The stars through clouds are peeping
                         They're saying the world should be sleeping
                         That means
                         Good-night
                         Sweet dreams.

(*Speaking*) Are you asleep?
**Jack** Nearly.
**Mrs Macdonald** (*to the audience, whispering*) Come on, help me sing him to
sleep. (*She leads the audience in the song, feeding them line by line*)

(*Singing*)              The moon his watch is keeping
                         The stars through clouds are peeping
                         They're saying the world should be sleeping
                         That means
                         Good-night
                         Sweet dreams.

(*Whispering*) Are you asleep?

*No reaction from Jack*

(*To the audience*) Thank you.
**Jeannie** Mum . . . I can't sleep.
**Mrs Macdonald** Why not, Jeannie.
**Jeannie** I keep hearing people singing.
**Mrs Macdonald** (*to the audience, whispering*) Once more, please, and we'll
send Jeannie off to sleep too. (*She leads the audience in the song again*)

(*Singing*)              The moon his watch is keeping
                         The stars through clouds are peeping
                         They're saying the world should be sleeping
                         That means
                         Good-night
                         Sweet dreams.

*She checks both children are asleep. Jack snores. Mrs Macdonald gives a
thumbs-up sign to the audience and mouths a "thank you". She gets into her
own bed*

(*To the audience, whispering*) Nightie-night!
**Audience** (*whispering*) Nightie-night!

## Music 6A

*The farmhouse revolves back to the exterior and the lighting changes*

SCENE 5

*The Farmyard. Night*

*After a pause,,to exciting, mysterious Music (6A continued), a baked bean tin tree begins to grow. It is all silver, and shimmers magically in the dim lighting. Instead of leaves, the tree has baked bean tins. The tree grows and grows*

*As it reaches higher and higher, Dog emerges from his kennel and sees it. He registers concern, and barks up at the farmhouse bedroom window*

*Jack pops his head out. He looks, amazed, at the tree, which continues to grow. He beckons inside, and Jeannie joins him at the window. They watch the tree grow out of sight up into the sky*

**Jack** (*awestruck*) It's a baked bean tin tree.
**Jeannie** (*amazed*) Your boosters *were* special after all.
**Jack** I *knew* Beep and Buzz wouldn't cheat me.

*He starts climbing out of the window on to the tree. (*NB*: If this is impracticable, Jack and Jeannie should have come out of the front door to see the tree; now Jack simply starts climbing the tree)*

**Jeannie** Where are you going?
**Jack** Where do you think?
**Jeannie** What will Mum say?
**Jack** Well, she said something would turn up. And it has! The tree's trying to help us; it knows we've got a problem and it's leading us to the answer. I've got to climb up, I've got to!
**Jeannie** Why?
**Jack** Why do people climb a mountain? Because it's there! I've got to go. To make up for losing Marigold ...

*Dog barks and starts climbing the tree*

Come on then, Dog, if you want to.

*They climb*

**Jeannie** Good luck, Jack!
**Jack** Thanks.
**Jeannie** Take care of each other!

*Music 6A continues as they climb higher as Jeannie watches. The scene begins to change*

SCENE 6

*Cloud Cuckoo Land*

*If possible, the scene change takes place in full view, or at least while Jack and Dog are in full view, isolated, perhaps, in follow spots*

*It should appear that they climb up and up until they arrive amongst the clouds these could be large cut-outs flown in, with dry ice billowing from beneath. Jack and Dog look about in great excitement. The music leads into ...*

### Song 6B: Cloud Cuckoo Land (Reprise)

**Jack**                    I've got my
                            Head in the clouds
                            My feet off the ground
                            My nose in the air
                            I've got my
                            Head in the clouds
                            I seem
                            To be in a dream.

*Suddenly, from behind the clouds, all around Jack and Dog, appear the singing Cloud Cuckoos, who proceed to accompany the song as a backing group*

(*Speaking*) Who are you?
**Cuckoos** Cuckoo! Cuckoo!
**Jack** Cuckoo! Then I must be in Cloud Cuckoo Land!
**Cuckoos** Cuckoo! Cuckoo!

(*Singing*)          Cuckoo! Cuckoo!
                    Cuckoo! Cuckoo!

                    Cuckoo! Cuckoo!
                    Cuckoo! Cuckoo!

| **Jack** | **Cuckoos** |
|---|---|
| Cloud Cuckoo Land is for dreamers | Cuckoo Cuckoo |
|  | Cuckoo Cuckoo |
| Dreamers with plenty to do | Cuckoo Cuckoo |
|  | Cuckoo Cuckoo |
| Cloud Cuckoo Land | Ah |
| Is the land | Cuckoo |
| For me | Cuckoo Cuckoo |
| Where maybe my dreams will come true. | Cuckoo |
| Cloud Cuckoo Land | Ah |
| Is the land | Cuckoo |
| For me | Ah |
| Where maybe my dreams will come true. | Cuckoo |

*The song ends as Jack and Dog start to climb again, watched by the Cloud Cuckoos, who wave farewell*

CURTAIN

**Entr'acte**

# ACT II

## SCENE 1

*Mrs Macdonald's farmyard*

*The baked bean tin tree is still there. The Pigs and Ducks are noisily awaiting their morning feed*

*Jeannie busily enters with two buckets*

*They cluster round her pushing and grunting and quacking*

**Jeannie** Come and get it! Pigs first. (*She pours pigswill in the trough*) That's all there is left. Don't gobble it.

*The Pigs take no notice and push and shove*

Here you are ducks. (*She feeds them by hand from the other bucket*) This is the last handful. Sorry.

*Resentful quacks*

*Mrs Macdonald enters from the farmhouse just as Jeannie starts to exit*

**Mrs Macdonald** (*yawning*) Sorry, dearie, I must have overslept. What are you doing?
**Jeannie** Just going to do some karate, Mum.
**Mrs Macdonald** Going to a party? At this time of the morning?
**Jeannie** Karate, Mum. I'm just going to practise my karate.
**Mrs Macdonald** But girls can't do karate. (*To the audience*) Can they?
**Audience** Yes!
**Mrs Macdonald** Oh no they can't!
**Audience** Oh yes they can!
**Mrs Macdonald** Can't!
**Audience** Can!
**Mrs Macdonald** Just checking. (*To Jeannie*) Have a nice time, dearie. Don't knock down too many brick walls.

*Jeannie exits*

*Mrs Macdonald has not yet noticed the baked bean tin tree*

(*To herself*) Karate! What next! Morning, pigs.

*The Pigs snort from the trough*

Morning, ducks.

*The Ducks quack. Mrs Macdonald suddenly notices the audience*                    .

Oh! *You're* still here! Good-morning.

**Audience** Good-morning.

**Mrs Macdonald** Good-mor—(*operatic flourish*)—ning.

**Audience** Good-mor—(*hopefully echo*)—ning.

**Mrs Macdonald** I'm so sorry we've rather neglected you. But it's been all
go. It's all go today, too. All go I know not where. Thanks to Mr Meany.
(*She has an idea*) I know, why doesn't Jack Mac show you his rocket?
what would pass a fun-filled couple of seconds. (*She calls*) Ja—ck! Jack
Mac!

*No response*

(*To the audience*) Give him a shout with me, eh? One, two, th——

*Hopefully some of the audience will point out to Mrs Macdonald that Jack is
not around. If not, after the shout, Mrs Macdonald should say, "Where is he?"*

What? He's not here? Where is he?

*The audience tell her about the tree*

Up the tree? What tree?

*She gets them to say "baked bean tin tree"*

Baked bean tin tree! (*She laughs*) You're having me on! Where is it?

*The audience shout "Behind you" and point, etc*

No! Never! Give over! ... *etc.*

*Finally ...*

There's no baked bean tin tree here ... (*She turns, sees it ...*)
Aaaaaaaaah! (*She faints and lies flat out on the ground*)

*The Ducks and Pigs immediately gather round her, concerned*

**Duck** (*trying to wake her*) Quack, quack, quack.

*No response. Pig approaches her and starts licking her face, snorting and
grunting*

**Mrs Macdonald** (*coming round*) Ah! Oh! (*Opening her eyes*) Ugh! Stop it,
Pig, I've had a wash this morning. (*Suddenly remembering*) Ooh, I've just
had a terrible turn. I turned and it was terrible. I thought I saw ...
(*confidential*) ... a b-b-baked tin bean tree.

*Duck quacks as if to say "A what?"*

I mean a b-b-bean tin baked tree.

*Pig snorts as if to say "A what?"*

I mean a tin bean tree baked.

*Duck quacks and Pig snorts as if to say "A what?"*

I mean ...

### Song 7: A Baked Bean Tin Tree

(*Singing*)          A baked bean tin tree
                    What a surprise
                    A baked bean tin tree
                    Reaching up to the skies
                    It grew in the night
                    It gave me a fright
                    But I must admit
                    It's a wonderful sight
                    To see
                    A baked bean tin tree.

**All**              A baked bean tin tree
**Mrs Macdonald**    Covered in tins
**All**              A baked bean tin tree
**Mrs Macdonald**    I'll have one for me dins!
                    A magical mys——
                    —t'ry puzzling as this
                    Is bound to confound
                    Horticultural his——
                    —tory
**All**              A baked bean tin tree.

**Mrs Macdonald**    There are seven wonders in the world
                    I've heard the experts state
                    But today those seven wonders
                    Have been joined by number eight!
**All**              Wonder number eight!

                    A baked bean tin tree
                    What a surprise
                    A baked bean tin tree
                    Reaching up to the skies
                    It grew in the night
                    It gave me a fright
                    But I must admit
                    It's a wonderful sight
                    To see
                    A baked bean
                    What does it mean?
                    A baked bean
                    I've never seen
                    A baked bean tin tree.

*At the end of the song . . .*

**Mrs Macdonald** Now, where were we? Ah yes. Jack. (*Suddenly remembering with horror*) The tree! (*To the audience*) You told me Jack had climbed up it, didn't you?
**Audience** Yes.
**Mrs Macdonald** (*to the Ducks and Pigs*) Is this true?

*They nod and quack/snort*

The great pudd'n'. Anything might happen to him. He might fall. Or get stuck up there . . . oh dearie, dearie, dearie me. What's to do?
**Duck** Quack, quack. (*As if to say, "You climb up after him"*)
**Mrs Macdonald** What? Me go up there?

*Duck quacks*

And find him?

*Pig snorts*

But I couldn't. I can't stand heights. Anyway, (*coyly*) girls can't climb trees. (*To the audience*) Can they?
**Audience** Yes!
**Mrs Macdonald** Oh no they can't!
**Audience** Oh yes they can!
**Mrs Macdonald** Oh no they can't!
**Audience** Oh yes they can!
**Mrs Macdonald** Oh! My knees have gone all knobbly, I mean wobbly. I can't do it. I can't.

*Suddenly Duck spots something off-stage. She quacks and points off*

What? (*She looks. She hears a voice*)
**Mr Meany** (*off*) Mrs Macdonald!
**Mrs Macdonald** It's Mr Meany. He's early. He's rum for his kent, I mean come for his rent! Ooh! Mr Meany! He's . . . (*She looks at the tree*) What am I waiting for? Bye ducks, bye pigs! (*She starts to climb*)

### Music 7A: Underscore/Chase music

*The Ducks and Pigs watch*

**Mr Meany** (*off*) Mrs Macdonald! Dear lady!

*When Mrs Macdonald is almost out of sight, Mr Meany enters, breathless*

Mrs Mac . . . (*breaths*) . . . don (*breaths*) . . . ald. (*He sees her up the tree*) She's trying to avoid me, the wretched woman. (*He calls*) Mrs Macdonald. Come back! How dare you try to escape me! I'll get you! I'll get you!

*He starts to climb too. The Pigs and Ducks watch*

*When Mr Meany is half-way up, Jeannie enters*

**Jeannie** (*calling*) Mum! (*She looks around and sees she is not there*) Mum!

*The audience will probably shout out, to tell Jeannie what has happened. If not she should ask them "Where is she?"*

(*Amazed*) Up there?

*The audience convince Jeannie that Mrs Macdonald is up the tree. Jeannie starts to climb as well. The Pigs and Ducks watch. The Lights fade as the music swells*

## SCENE 2

*The Grounds of the Silver Palace*

*In the land at the top of the baked bean tin tree, the predominant colour is silver. The huge silver gates to the palace tower above silver trees and/or shrubs. If possible, the top of the baked bean tin tree is visible, peeping from a stage trap or even the orchestra pit. (NB: The whole set for this scene needs to be quite well downstage, in order to accommodate the scene change.) The gates have widely-spaced bars. Through them it could be possible to see, on a front cloth, a path leading to the silver castle*

### Music 7B: Incidental Music

*After a short pause, Jack appears, climbing up the very top of the tree. Dog follows close behind*

*They tentatively look around, see the gates and decide to go through. They gingerly push a gate, which creaks eerily open just sufficient to creep through. Suddenly they are halted in their tracks by a noise—a mooing noise—a familiar mooing noise! They look around, as suddenly, from behind a bush or tree . . .*

*Marigold becomes visible*

*The audience probably shout out to help Jack and Dog find her, which they do without too much difficulty*

**Jack** (*whispers*) Marigold!

*They dash to her and affectionately greet her, then notice she is tied up— a silver loop round her neck, the end tied to the gate. Jack slips the loop off, and he and Dog lead her out of the gates, towards the top of the baked bean tin tree. Dog is delighted to see his best friend again*

Do you want to come home?

*Marigold moos affirmatively, nodding*

Good. Can you climb trees? Down not up.

*He shows her the treetop. Marigold moos negatively, shaking her head*

Come on, have a go.

*Suddenly all freeze as they hear voices*

**Beep** |                  | *Beep. Beep. Beep. Beep.*
**Buzz** | *(off, together)* | *Buzz. Buzz. Buzz. Buzz.*

*Jack and Dog quickly decide to hide, and reassure Marigold before dashing off or concealing themselves behind a bush*

### Music 7C: Entrance/Chase Music

*Buzz and Beep enter, upstage of the gates, Buzz carries a silver bucket*

**Beep** *Beep.* (*Calling*) Marigold.
**Buzz** *Buzz.* (*Calling*) Milktime.

*They stop abruptly when they see the gate ajar and Marigold not where they expected. They find the tethering rope*

**Beep** She's gone! *Beep.* Action stations!
**Buzz** Emergency! *Buzz.* Emergency!

*They dash about, getting in each other's way*

**Beep** *Beep.* Action stations.
**Buzz** Emergency! *Buzz.* Emergency!

*Suddenly they see Marigold outside the gates*

**Beep** *Beep.* There she is.

*They speed outside the gates to Marigold*

*Beep. Beep. Beep.*
**Buzz** *Buzz. Buzz. Buzz.* Emergency over.

*They lead her to a position in which they can replace the tether loop, but do not yet go inside the gates*

**Beep** *Beep.* Were you attempting escape, Marigold?

*Marigold moos an indeterminate moo*

*Beep.* We want Marigold to be happy.
**Buzz** Yes. *Buzz.* We want Marigold to make us buckets and buckets of milk. *Buzz.* Please.

*He politely puts the bucket down in front of Marigold. Beep and Buzz both step back and watch expectantly. Marigold looks at them*

*Buzz.* Milk, please, Marigold.

*Marigold looks at them as though they are crazy. We realize they do not know how to milk her*

**Beep** Do as you're told, disobedient cow. *Beep.* Milk.

*Still Marigold stands diffidently. Buzz picks up the bucket and holds it under Marigold's mouth, clearly expecting it to come from there*

**Buzz** (*cajoling*) Come on. *Buzz.* Good girl. *Buzz.* Good girl.

*No reaction*

**Beep** *Beep. Beep.* I have an idea.

*He goes to Marigold's rear. Buzz still holds the bucket under her mouth.
Beep picks up Marigold's tail and starts pumping it up and down*

(*In rhythm*) Milk. *Beep.* Please. *Beep.* Milk. *Beep.* Please. (*Eventually,
giving up in frustration*) *Beep! Beep! Beep!* (*Shouting*) Stupid cow! Stupid
cow! Stu——

*Jack suddenly emerges*

**Jack** There's no need to shout at her. (*He strokes her*) It's all right,
Marigold.

*Beep and Buzz react surprised to see him*

**Beep** *Beep.* what are *you* doing here?
**Buzz** *Buzz.* How did you get here?
**Jack** Not by rocket, thanks to you two. Those extra boosters weren't extra
boosters at all. They were baked beans. Mum threw them in the farmyard
and they grew into a baked bean tin tree. I climbed it and here I am.
**Beep** *Beep.* Buzz.
**Buzz** *Buzz.* Yes, Beep.
**Beep** You silly spaceman. *Beep.* You didn't give him extra boosters. *Beep.*
You gave him our *tea.*
**Buzz** *Buzz.* Sorry Beep. Apologies, friendly being.

*Suddenly they are interrupted by a very loud, booming voice; it is coming from
some way away, but is still pretty frightening*

**Silver Giant** (*off*) Where's—my—milk? Beep! Buzz! Where's my milk?

*Beep and Buzz are affected seriously by the voice, and show signs of panic*

**Jack** (*awestruck*) Who was that?
**Buzz** *Buzz. Buzz.* The Silver G-g-g-g-g-g-giant!
**Beep** *Beep.* He wants his milk.
**Buzz** (*picking up the bucket*) And we haven't got him any! *Buzz. Buzz. Buzz.*
He'll k-k-k-k-k-kill us.
**Beep** *Beep.* Control, Buzz. Control. Stabilize. Stabilize.

*Buzz calms down*

(*To Jack*) Please, friendly being, help us. *Beep.* Marigold was your cow.
Ask her to give us some milk. *Beep.* Please.
**Jack** Well, I . . .
**Beep** *Beep.* In return I promise extra boosters for your rocket.
**Jack** Yes, but . . .
**Silver Giant** (*off*) Where's—my—milk?
**Buzz** (*trembling*) Please! *Buzz.* Please!
**Jack** Oh, very well. Come on, Marigold.

*Tension rumble as he takes the bucket, places it under Marigold, then kneels down and starts milking her. Beep and Buzz gaze, astonished. It might be possible for the pantomime cow to be fitted with a milk container, so that "real" milk can be delivered into the bucket. But if Jack angles himself between Marigold and the audience, the effect can of course be cheated. Eventually, Jack holds up the bucket of milk*

There. Good girl, Marigold.

**Beep** *Beep.* Excellent.

**Buzz** *Buzz.* Brilliant.

**Jack** Why does the Silver Giant want milk?

**Beep** No time for that now. *Beep.* Let's go.

*Beep and Buzz take an arm each and lead Jack off through the gates*

**Jack** No! *I'm* not coming. Let me go!

**Beep** Forward. *Beep. Beep. Beep. Beep. Beep.*

**Buzz** *Buzz. Buzz. Buzz. Buzz. Buzz.*

*They exit, Jack protesting*

*Marigold is left, shaking her head in bewilderment. Suddenly Dog emerges from hiding. Dog removes the loop from round Marigold's neck. Marigold is very sad. Dog tries to cheer her up. Perhaps he does an acrobatic trick. Marigold hardly reacts. Dog woofs. Marigold moos. After a short exchange, the woofs and moos become rhythmical and lead into . . .*

### Song 8: Woof Moo-oo!

*During the song Marigold cheers up*

| | |
|---|---|
| **Dog** | Woof |
| **Marigold** | Moo-oo |
| **Dog** | Woof |
| **Marigold** | Moo-oo |
| **Dog** | Woof |
| **Marigold** | Moo-oo |
| **Dog** | Woof woof woof. |

| | |
|---|---|
| **Marigold** | Moo-oo |
| **Dog** | Woof |
| **Marigold** | Moo-oo |
| **Dog** | Woof |
| **Marigold** | Moo-oo |
| **Dog** | Woof |
| **Marigold** | Moo-oo. |

*Dance*

| | |
|---|---|
| **Dog** | Woof |
| **Marigold** | Moo-oo |

*Dance*

| | |
|---|---|
| **Marigold** | Moo-oo |
| **Dog** | Woof. |

| **Marigold** | Moo-oo |
| **Dog** | Woof woof |
| **Marigold** | Moo-oo |
| **Dog** | Woof woof |
| **Marigold** | Moo-oo |
| **Dog** | Woof |
| **Marigold** | Moo |
| **Dog** | Woof |
| **Marigold** | Moo |
| **Dog** | Woof woof. |

| **Dog** | Woof woof |
| **Marigold** | Moo-oo |
| **Dog** | Woof woof |
| **Marigold** | Moo-oo |
| **Dog** | Woof woof |
| **Marigold** | Moo |
| **Dog** | Woof |
| **Marigold** | Moo |
| **Dog** | Woof |
| **Marigold** | Moo moo. |

| **Dog** | Woof woof woof woof woof |
| **Marigold** | Moo-oo! |

*At the end of the song, Mrs Macdonald is seen struggling up to the top of the tree*

*Dog sees her and rushes to help her*

**Mrs Macdonald** Oh, Dog, am I glad to see you? Where's Jack?

*Marigold moos. Mrs Macdonald sees her*

Marigold. (*Mrs Macdonald rushes to embrace her. Tearful*) It's lovely to see you, you silly old cow. (*Suddenly*) How on earth did you get up here? I know the cow jumped over the moon, but this is ridiculous!

*She is interrupted by the booming voice of the Giant*

**Silver Giant** (*off*) Where's—my—milk? Where's—my—milk?
**Mrs Macdonald** Oo er! What's that?

*Dog mimes a giant*

What? (*To the audience*) What's Dog saying?

*She gleans from the audience the fact that it is the Silver Giant calling out*

The Silver Giant?
**Audience** Yes.
**Mrs Macdonald** Who's he when he's at home? (*Suddenly*) Is that where my Jack's gone?

*Dog barks. Marigold moos*

Come on, Dog. We'd better give him a hand. You stay there, Marigold. (*Calling*) Jack, Jack, it's all right dear. Mummy coming!

### Music 8A: Exit/Scene Change Music

*Mrs Macdonald and Dog exit, towards the palace. Marigold watches*

SCENE 3

*Inside the Silver Palace*

*The predominant colour is silver again. The room is clearly that of a giant. On one side is an oversize table and chair. On it sit large moneybags and a money box. On the other side there is, half onstage, half off, a large cage-like object, resembling a giant baby's playpen, which is in fact what it is. There are no windows, but a high door. The room is bigger than the area visible, so the Silver Giant will be able to enter, as it were, from the wings behind his table*

*Music as the door opens and Beep pops his head round. He leads in Jack, carrying the silver bucket, and Buzz*

**Beep** (*softly, as they enter*) *Beep. Beep.*
**Buzz** (*softly, as they enter*) *Buzz. Buzz.*
**Jack** (*rather loud*) Where are we?
**Beep** ⎫ (*together*) ⎱ Shhhhhhh!
**Buzz** ⎭             ⎰
**Beep** *Beep.*
**Buzz** *Buzz.*
**Beep** (*in a loud whisper*) The Silver Giant's Silver Palace. *Beep.* Buzz. Tell the boss we're back.
**Buzz** (*knees knocking*) *Buzz. Buzz.* I'd rather not.
**Beep** (*pushing him*) *Beep.* Go on.
**Buzz** (*pushing him*) *Buzz.* No, you go.
**Beep** *Beep.* You go.
**Buzz** *Buzz.* You go.
**Jack** (*rather loud*) *I'll* go.
**Beep** ⎫ (*together, grabbing Jack*) ⎱ Shhhhhhhhh!
**Buzz** ⎭                            ⎰
**Beep** *Beep!*
**Buzz** *Buzz!* *You* can't go.
**Jack** Why not?
**Beep** (*ominously*) *Beep.* The Silver Giant has a club.
**Jack** I'll join it. Do I get a badge?
**Buzz** No, no, *buzz.* Not that sort of club.
**Beep** (*fearfully*) *Beep.* The Silver Giant *swings* his club.
**Jack** Oh! A golf club!
**Beep** No, no, *Beep.* He ——

*They are interrupted by the booming voice of the Silver Giant from off-stage*

**Silver Giant** (*off*) Who—is—there? I—hear—voices. Who—is—there?

*Beep and Buzz are galvanized into action. Buzz climbs on to the chair, helped—given a leg up by—Beep. This could become a short comedy routine as Buzz slips, treads on Beep etc. All the time the Silver Giant's booming mutterings inspire fear and speed. Eventually Buzz gets on to the chair, and from there on to the table. He summons up courage, then shouts off into the wings*

**Buzz** (*nervous*) *Buzz*. Back, we're boss! Back, we're boss!

*Beep, below, nearly has a seizure*

(*Realizing*) Correction. *Buzz*. Boss, we're back! Boss, we're back.

*The Silver Giant grunts, off*

**Beep** (*prompting from below*) *Beep*. Mission trip success.
**Buzz** *Buzz*. What?
**Beep** (*in a loud whisper*) *Beep*. Tell him. Mission trip success.
**Buzz** *Buzz*. Right. (*He shouts off*) Fish and chips are best.

*The Silver Giant grunts interrogatively, off*

*Buzz*. Fish and chips are best.
**Beep** *Beep*. No!
**Buzz** *Buzz*. (*He shouts off*) No!

*The Silver Giant grunts interrogatively, off*

Correction. *Buzz*. Fish and chips are *not* best.
**Beep** *Beep*. Twit!
**Buzz** (*shouting off*) *Buzz*. Twit!

*The Silver Giant grunts angrily, off*

**Beep** *Beep*. Shut up!
**Buzz** (*shouting off*) *Buzz*. Shut up!

*The Silver Giant grunts more angrily, off*

**Beep** (*desperate*) *Beep*. Apologize.
**Buzz** *Buzz*. What?
**Beep** *Beep*. Apologize.
**Buzz** (*sincerely, to Beep*) *Buzz*. I'm sorry.
**Beep** Not to me. *Beep*. To *him*.
**Buzz** Oh. (*He shouts off*) I'm sor——

*Roars from the Silver Giant indicate he is on his way*

*Buzz*. *Buzz*. *Buzz*. He's coming! (*He stays on the table*)

### Music 8B: Entrance Music

*The Silver Giant enters. He should be as big as possible, but able to walk in a*

*shuffling manner. He looks exactly like a traditional fairy-tale story-book
giant, with beard and belt and club; but he is silver—at least, the
predominant colour is silver*

*He wields his club menacingly. Buzz, on the table, has to back away to avoid
being swept off. The Silver Giant should have a booming voice, which could
involve a radio mike, or even a ghosted voice into a microphone off-stage. But
in any event, the voice must be clear, not muffled. When the reaction to his
entry has died down . . .*

**Silver Giant** Well?
**Beep** (*shouting up*) *Beep.* Well what, Boss?
**Silver Giant** Where—are—these—fish and chips?
**Beep** *Beep.* Ah. Buzz didn't really say fish and chips, boss.
**Silver Giant** He—did! I—heard—him. I—fancy—fish and chips.
**Beep** No. He said "Mission trip success", boss. *Beep.* "Mission trip——"

*He is interrupted as the Silver Giant starts sniffing . . .*

**Silver Giant** (*sniff, sniff, sniff; then, with a roar*)
        Fee, fi, fo, fum
        I can smell that a *stranger's* come . . .
**Beep** Yes. Yes. *Beep.* Here he is! *Beep.* (*He pushes Jack forward*)
**Jack** How do you do? (*As a polite afterthought*) Sir.

*The Silver Giant raises his club*

**Silver Giant** I—*do*—very—well,—stranger. I'll—do—*you* . . . (*He goes to
    club Jack*)
**Beep** Stop!

*The Silver Giant stops*

    Boss, don't club this boy. *Beep.* I'm sure you'd like him.
**Silver Giant** Not as much as I'd like fish and chips. Still, maybe fried in
    batter or boiled in oil . . .
**Jack** (*realizing*) Hey, you can't eat me!
**Silver Giant** Can't I?
**Jack** No. I've brought you your milk . . . er, sir.
**Silver Giant** Milk? *Milk?* You have brought me *milk?*
**Jack** Yes sir. (*He shows the Silver Giant the bucket*)
**Silver Giant** It's a miracle!
**Jack** No, sir, it's milk.
**Silver Giant** I know it's milk, foolish boy. The fact that you have brought it
    is a miracle. What's your name?
**Jack** Jack Mac, sir.
**Silver Giant** And to think I nearly took you for a snack, Jack Mac. Forgive
    me. You are welcome.
**Jack** Thank you, sir.
**Silver Giant** (*starting to exit*) Treat—him—well, Beep and Buzz, treat—
    him—well.
**Jack** Oh, but . . . sir!

**Silver Giant** (*stopping*) Yes, Jack Mac?

**Jack** Aren't you going to *drink* the milk?

**Silver Giant** What? (*Suddenly he laughs*) Ho, ho, ho, ho. Foolish boy. The milk is not for *me*.

**Jack** (*looking at Beep and Buzz*) But I thought ...

**Silver Giant** No, no. The milk is for my son. You see, my wife ... er ... had to go on holiday, and left me in charge ...

*From off-stage, a wail. Baby Giant is awake! Immediately Beep and Buzz nervously spring into action*

**Beep** *Beep*. Boss! He's woken up!

*Another screaming wail*

**Buzz** *Buzz*. He's coming!

### Music 8C: Entrance Music

*Baby Giant enters. He is in his playpen, and can look through the bars. He is screaming. Played by an actor of average height, he is dressed in a silver nappy or "babygrow". Round his neck is a ribbon with a large silver dummy attached. He carries a baby's rattle-type object, in the shape of a giant's club—a miniature version of his father's*

*The Baby Giant's raucous screaming drives everyone mad; Jack watches fascinated as the Silver Giant covers his ears. Meanwhile, in an attempt to quieten him down, Beep and Buzz gingerly approach the playpen; Beep manages to grab the dummy and stuff it in Baby Giant's mouth; Buzz finds a silver teddy bear and dangles it over the bars. All this is under constant threat of being clubbed by Baby Giant. Nobody should get hit yet, however. The dummy calms Baby Giant down somewhat and the noise is reduced. The above sequence should not be rushed; Baby Giant's entrance and the devastating effect he has on the others, making conversation impossible and behaving like a savage caged beast is very necessary to set up the importance of Jack's "nursemaid" job*

**Jack** (*shouting*) Is he always like this?

**Silver Giant** You wait till he's woken up *properly*!

### Song 9: The Silver Giant's Lament

| | |
|---|---|
| (*Singing*) | Now when I became a father |
| | I got rather a surprise |
| | 'Cos no-one ever warned me |
| | Just how much a baby cries |

| | |
|---|---|
| **Baby Giant** | Waaa! Waaa! Waaa! |
| **Silver Giant** | Won't you stop that noise! |
| **Baby Giant** | Waaa! Waaa! Waaa! |
| **Silver Giant** | Won't you play with your toys? |
| **Baby Giant** | Waaa! Waaa! Waaa! |
| **Silver Giant** | You're driving me wild! |

| | |
|---|---|
| **Baby Giant** | Waaa! Waaa! Waaa! |
| **Silver Giant** | You horrible child! |

When I try to count my money
Like, most other giants do
It isn't very funny
Hearing Baby yell boo hoo!

| | |
|---|---|
| **Baby Giant** | Waaa! Waaa! Waaa! |
| **Silver Giant,** **Beep, Buzz** | Won't you stop that noise! |
| **Baby Giant** | Waaa! Waaa! Waaa! |
| **Silver Giant,** **Beep, Buzz** | Won't you play with your toys? |
| **Baby Giant** | Waaa! Waaa! Waaa! |
| **Silver Giant** | You're driving me spare |
| **Baby Giant** | Waaa! Waaa! Waaa! |
| **Silver Giant** | It just isn't fair! |

I try to make him be
A happy little chappie
I bounce him on my knee
I change his little nappy
But however hard I try
I only make him cry, cry, cry!

| | |
|---|---|
| **Baby Giant** | Waaaaaaa! Waaaaaaa! |
| **Silver Giant** | Such a nervous wreck he makes me There's nothing I can do All through the night he wakes me Till I end up crying too! |
| **Silver Giant,** **Baby Giant** | Waaa! Waaa! Waaa! |
| **Silver Giant,** **Beep, Buzz, Jack** | Won't you stop that noise! |
| **Silver Giant,** **Baby Giant** | Waaa! Waaa! Waaa! |
| **Silver Giant,** **Beep, Buzz, Jack** | Won't you play with your toys? |
| **Silver Giant,** **Baby Giant** | Waaa! Waaa! Waaa! |
| **Silver Giant** | Be kind to your dad! |
| **Silver Giant,** **Baby Giant** | Waaa! Waaa! Waaa! |
| **Silver Giant** | You're driving me mad! |
| **All** | Waaa! Waaa! Waaa! |
| **Silver Giant** | You're driving me spare! |
| **All** | Waaa! Waaa! Waaa! |

| | |
|---|---|
| **Silver Giant** | It just isn't fair! |
| **All** | Waaa! Waaa! Waaa! |
| **Silver Giant** | You're driving me wild! |
| **All** | Waaa! Waaa! Waaa! |
| **Silver Giant** | You horrible child! |
| **All** | Waaaaaa! |

*At the end of the song, Baby Giant starts screaming again, even louder*

**Baby Giant** Waaaaaaaaaa! Um um um um um um umum!

*Beep shoves his dummy back in, gingerly approaching the playpen bars to do so. Loud sucking noises*

**Buzz** (*to Jack*) *Buzz.* This is why we needed Marigold and her milk so badly.
**Beep** *Beep.* The boss read about it in the *Baby Giant-Care Book.*
**Silver Giant** Give him some of your magic milk, Jack Mac.

*Jack looks at Beep and Buzz and they nod encouragement*

Beep—spoon.

*Beep fetches a giant spoon for Jack. Tension rumble as Jack approaches the playpen. He holds the bucket and spoon in front of him*

**Jack** (*in baby-talk voice*) Hallo, Baby Giant. There's a good little baby. I've got some nice milky-wilky for yousy-wousy! Look! (*He smacks his lips invitingly*)
**Baby Giant** (*suddenly, making the dummy shoot out*) Waaaaaaaaaaaa!

*Jack retreats a little, then advances once more. He puts the bucket down near the playpen, then dips in the spoon. He gingerly pushes a spoonful of milk through the bars. The others watch intently. What will Baby Giant do? Baby Giant espies the intruding spoon. He is interested. He changes his scream to a whimper. Suddenly he aims at the spoon with his club, as though to swipe it. But just as suddenly he stops and sniffs. He sniffs again. He likes the smell. He tries a taste. Loud sucking noises, following by lip-smacking tasting noises. Greedily he sucks up all the milk. Then, eagerly*

Umumumumumumumumumum!

*Jack scoops up more and passes the spoon in. Slurping sounds. Then, with great enthusiasm . . .*

Umumumumumumumumumum!

*As Jack goes to scoop another spoonful, Baby Giant grabs the bucket through the bars, lifts it up and uses it as a cup. Very loud drinking noises. He finishes it*

**Silver Giant** (*delighted*) He liked it!

*Beep and Buzz "applaud"*

| | | |
|---|---|---|
| **Beep** | (*together*) | Beep. Beep. Beep. Beep. |
| **Buzz** | | Buzz. Buzz. Buzz. Buzz. |

*Jack turns to them, pleased. Immediately Baby Giant turns the bucket over and drops it on Jack's head*

**Baby Giant** (*excited noises of pleasure*) Waa! Waa! Waa! Waa!

*The Silver Giant roars with laughter*

**Silver Giant** Ho, ho, ho, ho!

*Jack removes the bucket, a little stunned*

He likes you!

*Jack turns back to Baby Giant*

**Baby Giant** (*with a coy smile*) Gurgle, gurgle, gurgle.
**Silver Giant** And the milk's stopped him crying!
**Baby Giant** (*singing tunelessly*) La, la, la, la, la.
**Silver Giant** He's a *happy* Baby Giant!
**Beep** ⎫ (*together, smiling*) ⎧ *Beep.* Aaaaaaaaaah!
**Buzz** ⎭                    ⎩ *Buzz.* Aaaaaaaaaah!
**Silver Giant** Thank you, Jack Mac.
**Jack** That's all right, Silver Giant, sir. Well, I'd better be off now. (*He makes a move*)
**Silver Giant** What?

*Beep and Buzz react to the different tone. They "cover" the door*

**Jack** I'd er . . . I'd better go.
**Silver Giant** (*roaring*) Go? How can you go, you heartless boy? My baby likes you. He *needs* you.

*Baby Giant makes loving noises aimed at Jack*

**Jack** But my mother will be worried.
**Silver Giant** Your mother? But this poor baby has *no* mother.
**Jack** You said she was on holiday.
**Silver Giant** (*getting angry*) She might be away a long time.
**Jack** No, I'm sorry, I must . . .

*He goes towards the door. Beep and Buzz stop him. They lift him and carry him to the playpen*

No! Put me down!

*They lift him over the bars and into the playpen*

Aaaaaaaaah!
**Silver Giant** There you are, baby—a little friend to play with. Ho, ho, ho!

*Baby Giant hugs Jack and gives him a big slobbery kiss*

**Beep** ⎫ (*together, smiling*) ⎧ *Beep.* Aaaaaaaaaah!
**Buzz** ⎭                    ⎩ *Buzz.* Aaaaaaaaaah!
**Silver Giant** Now then, baby. It's time for your clubbing lesson.

*Baby Giant eagerly holds his club in readiness*

You remember what we learned last time?

*Baby Giant nods, eyes glinting*

Comfortable grip in both hands.

*Baby Giant arranges his grip*

Upward swing!

*Baby Giant swings the club over his head*

Check target.

*Baby Giant takes aim at Jack*

Downward swing!

*Baby Giant smashes the club down on Jack*

**Jack** Ow!
**Silver Giant** Not bad. But don't rush the follow-through. Watch me. I'll show you. (*He calls*) Buzz! Stand there.
**Buzz** *Buzz*. I'd rather not stand there, boss.
**Silver Giant** Stand there.
**Buzz** *Buzz*. Yes, boss. (*He does so, cringing in anticipation*)
**Silver Giant** (*demonstrating with his own club*) So, it's upward swing! Check target! Downward swing!

*He smashes Buzz, who reels*

**Buzz** *Buzz*. Ow!
**Silver Giant** Have another go, baby.

*Jack tries to hide, but is cornered by Baby Giant*

Upward swing! Check target!

*Jack is darting about, dodging from side to side*

Jack Mac stand *still*! Give him a chance. He's only a baby.

*Jack stops to protest*

**Jack** But . . .
**Silver Giant** Downward swing!

*Baby Giant bashes Jack again*

**Jack** Ow.
**Silver Giant** Excellent. Much better. Good baby. Good baby.
**Baby Giant** Gurgle, gurgle, gurgle.
**Jack** (*rubbing his head*) Look, sir, I really think I ought to go home. I didn't tell my mother I was coming and——
**Silver Giant** (*with a roar*) Quiet! How dare you upset my son.

*Tension rumble*

Understand, Jack Mac, you—will—not—leave—until my son is grown-up. Until then you—will—stay—here—and keep him company.

**Jack** But, sir——

**Silver Giant** (*with a roar*) Do you understand?

**Jack** Yes, sir.

**Baby Giant** Waaaaaaaaaaaaa!

**Silver Giant** See, you've frightened him now, you heartless monster. Beep, Buzz—more milk.

**Beep** } (*together*) { *Beep*. Yes, boss.
**Buzz** }           { *Buzz*. Yes, boss.

*They exit at speed, taking the bucket with them*

*Baby Giant wails spasmodically*

**Silver Giant** Now. I have to count my silver coins. (*He goes and sits at the table*) And I want no noise to interrupt my concentration. Do you understand, Jack Mac?

**Jack** Yes, sir.

**Baby Giant** Waaa!

**Silver Giant** I said "*no noise*". (*He settles to counting his silver*)

**Jack** Shhhhh! Baby, *please*.

**Baby Giant** Waaaaaaaa!

**Jack** Shhhhh! (*He pops the dummy in*)

**Baby Giant** (*spitting out the dummy*) Waaaaaaa!

*Jack pops the dummy in again*

(*Spitting it out again*) Waaaaaaa!

**Jack** Shhhh! I tell you what—I'll sing to you. All right?

**Baby Giant** Waaaaaaa!

### Song 9A: Sweet Dreams (Reprise)

**Jack**          The moon his watch is keeping
                  The stars through clouds are peeping
                  They're saying the world should be sleeping
                  That means
                  Good-night
                  Sweet Dreams.

**Baby Giant** Waaaaaaaa!

*The Baby Giant nods off to sleep and snores happily. Another louder, snore is heard. It is the Silver Giant, whose head now flops forward on to his arms*

**Jack** (*with a gasp*) I've nodded *him* off too! (*He looks about*) Time I was off. (*He gingerly starts trying to climb out of the playpen. If necessary he uses Baby Giant's club as a step. With great effort, he manages to climb up to the top*)

*Both Giants snore the while. Just as Jack is about to jump down from the top of the playpen . . .*

*The door bursts open and in rushes Mrs Macdonald, followed by Dog*

**Mrs Macdonald** (*seeing Jack, shouting*) Have no fear, dear, Mother's here!

*Dog barks, as if to say "Have no fear, Dog's here". Jack is distracted and topples back into the playpen*

**Jack** Oh, Mum, get out! And you, Dog.
**Mrs Macdonald** Charming.

*Dog barks indignantly*

Nearly break our necks getting here to get him out and he tells *us* to get out.

*Dog barks agreement*

**Jack** Shhhhh. *Please.*

*Suddenly Baby Giant and the Silver Giant stir. Silver Giant snores with a jolt*

**Baby Giant** Waa ... waa ...!

*Jack points them out to Mrs Macdonald and Dog*

**Mrs Macdonald** Oo er!
**Jack** (*in a loud whisper*) We'd just got them asleep when you came barging in.
**Mrs Macdonald** (*indignant*) Well, we weren't to know, cleverclogs. Were we, Dog?

*Dog barks agreement*

**Jack** Shhhhh!
**Baby Giant** (*waking*) Waaaaa, waaaaa!
**Jack** (*to the audience*) Quick! Will you help me, please? Get them to sleep again. "The moon his watch is keeping". Very quiet.

*When she realizes what is happening, Mrs Macdonald joins in. Dog barks along. Jack feeds lines to the audience as necessary*

| | |
|---|---|
| **Jack,** | The moon his watch is keeping |
| **Mrs Macdonald,** | The stars through clouds are peeping |
| **Dog, Audience** | They're saying the world should be sleeping |
| | That means |
| | Good-night |
| | Sweet dreams. |

*By the end of the song, Baby Giant is asleep again*

**Jack** (*in a whisper to the audience*) Thank you.

### Music 9B: Incidental/Chase/Fight Music

*In mime, Dog and Mrs Macdonald try to rescue Jack. Dog helps Mrs Macdonald up on to the top of the playpen. She sits astride it, and helps Jack up and over and down. Dog receives him*

*At that moment, Beep and Buzz enter with the bucket. They see what is going on*

**Beep** He's escaping. Emergency. *Beep. Beep. Beep.*
**Buzz** Alarm. Alarm. *Buzz. Buzz. Buzz.*

*After a slight panic, getting in each other's way, Beep puts down the bucket, and Buzz presses an alarm bell near the door. An alarm rings out. The Silver Giant and Baby Giant start to stir. Beep and Buzz advance on the horrified Jack and Dog, who back away, leaving Mrs Macdonald stuck on top of the playpen*

**Mrs Macdonald** (*screaming*) Help!

*A short chase, in which Beep chases Jack, and Buzz chases Dog, around table legs, through chair legs, between the legs of the sitting Giant, etc. At a crucial stage, when the two chases are coming towards each other, Jack and Dog sidestep; Beep and Buzz bash into each other, and fall over, stunned. Jack and Dog run towards the door, escaping. Mrs Macdonald calls them*

**Mrs Macdonald** Help!

*Baby Giant has woken up, and, unseen by Mrs Macdonald, advances on her, wielding his club. He swings, but aims incorrectly, smashing his club on to the top of the playpen*

**Baby Giant** (*furious*) Waaaaaa!
**Mrs Macdonald** (*seeing him*) Aaaaaaaah!

*As Baby Giant takes aim again, Jack dashes back to help Mrs Macdonald, who slips down on to his shoulders. Jack moves away, with her on top, just in the nick of time—a second later, Baby Giant's club smashes down on the spot where Mrs Macdonald had been. Beep and Buzz are still stunned*

**Baby Giant** Waaaaaaah!

*This finally wakes the Silver Giant, who turns, sees what is going on and stands*

**Silver Giant** (*roaring*) Aaaaaaaaaah!

*Mrs Macdonald is still sitting astride Jack's shoulders. Jack turns, causing Mrs Macdonald and the Silver Giant to be almost face to face*

**Mrs Macdonald** Aaaaaaaaaah!

*She vainly tries to punch the Silver Giant who simply takes her in a bear hug off Jack's shoulders. He swings her about or crushes her. Jack sees this, horrified. So does Dog, who has been holding the door open, ready for escape. Now he dashes back, and he and Jack attack the Giant's feet and ankles. Jack stamps on a foot, and Dog snaps at an ankle. This seems to have little or no effect. But Mrs Macdonald is struggling, and finally wriggles from the Silver Giant's bear hug, slipping down to the ground below, if possible falling on to Jack and Dog. She tries to get up, but has sprained her ankle, and starts to rub it vehemently*

*Beep and Buzz recover, and make a quick grab for Jack and Dog. They succeed in pinioning their arms behind them, and drag them, struggling, back towards the door. Beep takes Jack. Buzz takes Dog. This leaves Mrs*

*Macdonald helpless on the ground. The Silver Giant sees this and takes his club. Tension as he lifts the club above his head and smashes it down. Mrs Macdonald manages to roll out of the way. The club hits the ground. The Silver Giant takes aim again. He swings the club up. Then smashes it down. Mrs Macdonald manages to roll the other way. The Silver Giant misses her again*

*Suddenly the door bursts open, knocking over Beep and Jack plus Buzz and Dog. Mr Meany enters, breathless and angry. He sees Mrs Macdonald on the ground and goes straight to her*

**Mr Meany** There you are, Mrs Macdonald! How dare you try to escape from me——

*Bash! The Silver Giant has taken a third aim, and this time smashes the club down on Mr Meany's head*

Aaaaaaaaaah! (*He collapses*)

*Beep and Buzz extricate themselves from Jack and Dog, and run to Mr Meany. They haul him up and then struggle to tip him into the playpen to imprison him. Jack and Dog dash from the door and help Mrs Macdonald up. She puts one arm round each of them. As they lift her, hobbling, away from the battle-ground, the Silver Giant, roaring furiously, picks up some moneybags from the table and throws them at the retreating trio, narrowly missing them. As Mrs Macdonald, Jack and Dog reach the door, and as Beep and Buzz succeed in tipping the unconscious Mr Meany into the playpen . . .*

*Jeannie enters*

*The music reaches a climax and stops. The Silver Giant throws another money bag, which falls at Jeannie's feet. All freeze*

**Jeannie** (*to the Giant*) What on earth do you think you're doing, you great fat bully?
**Mrs Macdonald** Careful, dear.
**Silver Giant** (*roaring*) What? You little pipsqueak.
**Jeannie** You overgrown lump of gristle!
**Silver Giant** What?

*He advances. Jeannie prepares to fight him*

**Mrs Macdonald** What are you doing, Jeannie?
**Jeannie** I'm going to give this Giant a lesson he won't forget.
**Mrs Macdonald** But . . . but girls can't fight giants. (*To the audience*) Can they?
**Audience** Yes!
**Mrs Macdonald** Oh no they can't!
**Audience** Oh yes they can!
**Mrs Macdonald** Oh no they can't!
**Audience** Oh yes they can!
**Mrs Macdonald** Well, I hope you're right!

*Tense, exciting music (9B continued) for the big fight. This should be a choreographed set piece, in which the Giant uses his club as well as his hands; Jeannie uses karate moves. The fight should veer from one side to the other. But eventually, on her own, watched in awe by all the others, Jeannie is triumphant. The Silver Giant is knocked out or retires hurt shouting "I give in, I give in". Mrs Macdonald and Jack lead the cheering. Beep and Buzz rush to tend their master*

Well done, dearie. (*To the audience*) You *were* right!

**Jeannie** (*to the others*) Come on, quick!

*She picks up the bags of money, and gives one each to Mrs Macdonald, Jack, Dog and herself. She bundles them out of the door*

*Mr Meany wakes up—in the playpen. He sees them going*

**Mr Meany** Hey! What about me?

*Baby Giant lands a beautifully timed club on Mr Meany's head*

Aaaaaaaaah!

*Baby Giant chortles and gurgles happily and covers Mr Meany with sloppy kisses*

Help!

*Black-out*


## SCENE 4

*The Grounds of the Silver Palace*

*Through the darkness booms the voice of the Silver Giant*

**Silver Giant** (*off*) After them, you stupid spacemen. After them! Don't let them escape!

### Music 9C: Exciting Entrance Music

*The Lights come up*

*Through the silver gates appear Jeannie and Dog; they pause, waiting for Jack and Mrs Macdonald. Eventually they too appear; Mrs Macdonald is hobbling and being helped by Jack*

*They all look around, as though momentarily lost. They start going the wrong way—in the direction opposite the top of the baked bean tin tree. Then Jack realizes they are wrong, and points back to the tree. They start to climb down*

### Song 9D: A Baked Bean Tin Tree (Reprise)

| | |
|---|---|
| **Mrs Macdonald, Jeannie, Jack, (Dog)** | Down the baked bean tin tree<br>Quick as we can<br>Down the baked bean tin tree |

Back to where we began.
We'll come to no harm
If we can keep calm
One branch at a time
And back at the farm
We'll be,
Down the baked bean tin tree.

Down the baked bean tin tree
**Mrs Macdonald**       Mind how you go
**All**                 Down the baked bean tin tree
**Mrs Macdonald**       Take it gentle and slow
**All**                 It's ever so tall
Take care not to fall
Keep hanging on tight
And cross fingers we'll all
Get free.
Down the baked bean
**Mrs Macdonald**       We're going back
**All**                 Down the baked bean
**Jeannie, Jack**       Dog, Mrs Mac
**All**                 Down the baked bean
**(Dog), Mrs Macdonald** Jeannie and Jack
**All**                 Down the baked bean
We're going back
Down the baked bean tin tree.

*One starts to descend, but ...*

*Suddenly Beep and Buzz arrive*

**Beep** *Beep. Beep. Beep. Beep.*
**Buzz** *Buzz. Buzz. Buzz. Buzz.*

*They come through the gates, and advance on the escapers, who leave the tree and take the only possible course—through the auditorium*

### Music 9E: Chase Music

*A chase ensues through the auditorium, which can be as long or as short as the scene change dictates. At one point the escapers should hide amongst members of the audience, causing Beep and Buzz to go past them. Beep and Buzz could ask the audience where the escapers have gone; the audience send them off in the wrong direction—maybe out of the auditorium doors*

*Jack, Jeannie, Mrs Macdonald and Dog descend the tree*

*Beep and Buzz return, but reach the tree just too late—all four have descended. They express in mime their annoyance, and crossly go back in through the silver gates as though back to the Silver Palace*

*After a pause, Marigold enters, sadly. She has been left behind. She looks down the tree, shakes her head, and sadly wanders away*

*Black-out*


SCENE 5

*The Farmyard*

*The Lights come up on an empty farmyard. The baked bean tin tree is still there, of course*

*Pig and Piglets enter. They go to the feeding trough, but it is empty. Grunts of hunger and disappointment*

*Duck and Ducklings enter. They go to the farmhouse door, quacking for . food. No reaction*

*The hungry Pigs and Ducks all look at and up the baked bean tin tree and sigh. Sudden hoots of a horn interrupt them, and they scatter in all directions*

*In a ramshackle old-fashioned car—or, if this is impracticable, on a bicycle—Sergeant Sweet enters*

**Sergeant Sweet** Morning pigs, morning ducks.

*The Pigs grunt a welcome, the Ducks quack one. All gather round him eagerly, as he gets out of the car or dismounts from his bicycle*

I'm a teeny weeny bit late, I'm afraid. Mrs Macdonald in?

*The Pigs and Ducks grunt and quack "No"*

Oh, that's funny. Mr Meany here?

*The Pigs and Ducks grunt and quack "No". Sergeant Sweet sees the audience*

Ah, the visitors are still here. (*Shyly*) How do?

**Audience** How do?

*The Pigs grunt and the Ducks quack hungrily. They have surrounded Sergeant Sweet*

**Sergeant Sweet** What's up with you lot? Eh?

*More grunts and quacks*

(*To the audience*) What's the matter with 'em, eh?
**Audience** They're hungry.
**Sergeant Sweet** Hungry? Be you hungry?

*Grunts and quacks*

Oh dear. There's not much as I can do about that. Unless . . .

*The Pigs and Ducks look up at him eagerly*

(*Shyly*) Well, p'raps I could ... er ... sing you a song. That might take your mind off being hungry.

*Enthusiastic grunts and quacks*

Right. Well, let's see. I don't know as I knows many songs ... ah, I know. I'll give you one as I teach the boys and girls down at the village school. You see, a lot of 'em walk to school, and I like to think as how they'll be safe when they have to cross the road. There's a vast amount of nasty fast traffic streaming past that time of the morning. *And* in the afternoon when they goes home, too. Now, if Mr Meany has his way and you pigs and ducks have to leave the farm, happen you might have to cross a road, and you'd best know how to do it, hadn't you?

*Grunts and quacks*

Right then. Listen.

### Song 10: Use Your Eyes and Ears

*Sergeant Sweet sings the song, doing actions to suit the words*

(*Singing*)        Use your eyes and ears
Before you use your feet
Look and listen
Before you cross the street
Double check and when you're satisfied
Walk, don't run
To the other side.

(*Speaking*) Can you remember that?

*Grunts and quacks of uncertainty; the Pigs and Ducks hesitantly try the actions.* (NB: *Some directors may not want the animals to* sing *in human voices, in which case they can grunt and quack; some directors may feel that dramatic licence enables them to sing!*)

Mmm. Tell you what. Do you think the visitors might give us a hand? (*To the audience*) Would you help me teach the pigs and ducks the song?
**Audience** Yes.
**Sergeant Sweet** You would?
**Audience** Yes.
**Sergeant Sweet** Oh, thank you.

---

### OPTIONAL

Now, just by chance, I've got the songsheet I uses to teach the school children. (*He unrolls it, taking it from his car or bike*)

---

Now, we'll learn it a couple of lines at a time. And don't forget the actions. Why don't you all stand up?

*He teaches the audience the song in three chunks, repeating each one, with appropriate actions, a couple of times to ensure familiarity. It is advisable for him to do this without musical accompaniment. The standing up should not be forced, but encouraged*

Now, let's put it all together. After three. One, two, three . . .

*During this section, the Ducks and Pigs begin to get it right*

**Sergeant Sweet,** ⎫ Use your eyes and ears
**Audience**      ⎭ Before you use your feet
Look and listen
Before you cross the street
Double check and when you're satisfied
Walk don't run
To the other side.

**Sergeant Sweet** (*speaking*) Very good. (*To the animals*) How are you lot doing?

*The Pigs and Ducks look a little uncertain*

Let's have another go. One, two, three . . .
**All**                Use your eyes and ears
Before you use your feet
Look and listen
Before you cross the street
Double check and when you're satisfied
Walk don't run
To the other side

**Sergeant Sweet** (*speaking*) Excellent. One more time and the pigs and ducks'll be perfect! One, two, three . . .
**All**                Use your eyes and ears
Before you use your feet
Look and listen
Before you cross the street
Double check and when you're satisfied
Walk don't run
To the other side

**Sergeant Sweet** (*speaking to the audience*) Thank you. You can all sit down again!

*As he rolls up his songsheet, or as he congratulates the Pigs and Ducks, music as . . .*

*Mrs Macdonald, Jack, Jeannie and Dog come down the baked bean tin tree*

*The Pigs and Ducks see them coming, and cluster round. Sergeant Sweet watches in surprise*

**Mrs Macdonald** Morning, Sergeant. Sorry we're late. Morning, pigs, morning, ducks.

*Grunts and quacks. The animals crowd round Mrs Macdonald*

**Sergeant Sweet** What's going on, madam?
**Mrs Macdonald** Well, you see something came up overnight—this tree to be exact—and we've just been for a little climb.

*The others are down. Dog barks urgently and mimes chopping the tree down*

**Jack** What? Chop the tree down?
**Jeannie** He's right, Jack. Just in case you know who comes down.

*She dashes off to get the axe*

**Sergeant Sweet** (*mystified*) Be there ... er ... somebody else coming down the tree then?
**Mrs Macdonald** No, no Sergeant. (*With a smile*) We're all here ...

*Jeannie returns with two axes*

*She hands one to Jack; they start chopping the foot of the tree. Each chop is echoed musically. The tree tumbles down, over into the wings. All cheer*

Now, Sergeant Gorgeous.
**Sergeant Sweet** *Sweet*, madam.
**Mrs Macdonald** I know. Gorgeous Sergeant Sweet!
**Sergeant Sweet** Yes. Well. You know why I'm here, madam.
**Mrs Macdonald** Yes, Sergeant. You very kindly, nay (*relishing the pun*) *sweetly* ... gave us twenty-four hours to find the money.
**Jeannie** And we've found it!

*They all show the moneybags. Jack takes out some silver pieces*

**Sergeant Sweet** Oh, congratulations, madam. I'm delighted for you. Now all you have to do is give the money to Mr Meany. I wonder where he's got to.
**Jack** He's ——

*He starts to point upwards, but Mrs Macdonald stops him, with a knowing look*

**Mrs Macdonald** He's not *here*, by the look of it.
**Sergeant Sweet** No. (*He looks at his pocket-watch*) Mm. And the deadline passed some minutes ago.

*Pause. Sergeant Sweet thinks about what to do. The others look hopefully at him*

Well, now. This is how I sees it. I gave you twenty-four hours to find the money, which you have done, *and* give it to Mr Meany, which you have *not* done. So ...
**All** (*protesting*) But ... it's not our fault ... *etc.*
**Sergeant Sweet** Quiet!

*All settle*

So, as it is through no fault of your own that you haven't given it to Mr Meany, rather Mr Meany's own failure to turn up to receive it, I reckon the money be no longer payable and that Mrs Macdonald can keep it. (*To the audience*) Be that fair?

**Audience** Yes!

*All cheer*

*Sergeant Sweet quickly gets in his car or on his bicycle and exits waving and blowing his horn*

*All wave and shout "Bye" and "Thank you". Mrs Macdonald hugs Jack and Jeannie. Dog barks with pleasure*

**Mrs Macdonald** We don't have to leave the farm after all!

*Cheers. Mrs Macdonald happily beckons her "family" to her*

Jack! Jeannie! Dog! Ducks! Pigs! Marigold!

*Everything stops dead. The realization that Marigold has been left behind suddenly hits everybody. Pause. Then . . .*

Marigold! We forgot Marigold!

**Jack** We left her up there.

**Jeannie** With the Silver Giant.

**Mrs Macdonald** Marigold! (*She starts to cry. To herself*) It's no use crying, you great pudd'n'. *Do* something. (*She rushes to where the tree was*) I'm coming, Marigold! I'm coming to fetch you home . . . (*She goes to climb the tree, then realizes*) We chopped it down!

**Jack** (*guiltily*) Yes, Mum.

**Mrs Macdonald** Marigold's gone for ever! (*She starts to cry again*)

**Jeannie** There must be *something* we can do. Can't we get up there another way?

*Pause. Suddenly . . .*

**Jack** Got it! My rocket!

**Mrs Macdonald** Your rocket?

**Jack** My rocket. If Beep and Buzz travelled to the Silver Palace by spaceship, I can get there in my rocket.

**Mrs Macdonald** I'd like to see you try!

**Jack** All right. (*He starts towards the shack*)

**Mrs Macdonald** Hold your horses, I was joking. Your rocket wouldn't get off the ground let alone get up there! Your rocket copped it, remember?

**Jack** Yes, but . . . look! (*From inside his shirt he gingerly takes out two silver objects—similar but not the same shape as the baked bean tins*)

**Mrs Macdonald** What are those?

**Jack** Extra boosters. Real ones. Beep and Buzz gave them to me in return for milking Marigold. (*He looks eagerly at Mrs Macdonald*)

**Jeannie** Let him try, Mum.

**Mrs Macdonald** Well, I don't know. It's so risky.

**Jack** Please, Mum.

**Mrs Macdonald** You might get lost in outer space. Or meet a meteor. Or get drownded in the Milky Way. Or get set alight by a satellite!

**Jack** Think of Marigold, Mum.

**Mrs Macdonald** (*to the audience*) What do the visitors think? Should I let him go?

**Audience** Yes.

**Mrs Macdonald** But he's my only son. Should I let him go?

**Audience** Yes.

**Mrs Macdonald** Oh, all right then. Good luck, dearie.

*Jack kisses Mrs Macdonald goodbye and heads for the shack. The others all cluster together to watch—standing a fair distance from the shack*

*Jack goes into the shack and shuts the shack door*

*An expectant hush. Then the sound of an engine being turned over (rather like a car engine). It does not start. Pause. Another go. Again the engine doesn't start. Mrs Macdonald and the others look concerned. Another try. This time the engine bursts into life. Everyone cheers*

**Mrs Macdonald** (*leading the others, and the audience*) Ten, nine, eight, seven, six, five, four, three, two, one, zero!

*All shout "Good luck" as suddenly, with appropriate sound effects, the rocket bursts out of the top of the shack, and steadily progresses up and out of sight. As it appears, perhaps the walls of the shack collapse in a heap. Smoke or dry ice billows. Music rumbles, as the rocket disappears*

*Black-out*

SCENE 6

*Out in Outer Space*

*The presentation of this scene can really be as simple or as complicated as required. It could be most effectively done as a UV puppetry sequence; the actors could be used with the puppets, or not. Another possibility is a rod puppet silhouette mime, against a screen. Or even an animated cartoon projected on a screen. The basic storyline could be simplified or embroidered as budget and skills and circumstances dictate*

**Music 10A**

1. *The sky.* Jack's rocket travelling. He could pass or narrowly avoid other familiar flying objects—birds, an airship, an air balloon, a helicopter, aeroplanes—(Concorde?). At least one moment of danger or possible collision. Clouds? Rainbow?

2. *Space.* Jack's rocket in the stars. He could pass other space objects, such as a meteorite, a flying saucer (with, perhaps, a strange space creature sitting on it); a radio satellite; planets/moons in the distance; a lunar module.

3. *The Silver Planet.* Getting nearer, leading to a landing.

4. *The rescue.* Jack rescues Marigold. This could be done using actors or puppets. If the landing happened on stage level, we might see the silver gates of the palace, Jack emerging from the rocket, finding Marigold and escorting her on board.

5. *The near-miss.* At the critical moment, Beep and Buzz enter and nearly catch Marigold and prevent the escape. They angrily watch as Jack's rocket takes off again, then rush off (to take chase in their spaceship).

6. *The flight home.* Jack's rocket returning. Suddenly Beep and Buzz's spaceship in pursuit. Exciting chase, cat and mouse style, amid the stars.

7. *The black hole.* A menacing whirlpool in space, towards which Jack's rocket is forced by Beep and Buzz's spaceship. After several near misses, Jack's rocket escapes. But Beep and Buzz's spaceship is sucked into the black hole.

8. *More life or death drama!* Jack's rocket encounters a vast space craft with jaw-like hatches; it tries to "swallow" Jack's rocket like a shark swallowing a smaller fish. Menacing, flashing lights, etc. Eventual escape, and descent.

During the sequence, a series of sound effects, including spaceship/rocket noises, moos, beeps and buzzes, electronic sounds, etc. could be used to heighten and clarify the action. Music 10A should accompany throughout. The sequence should not be too long, but provide a theatrical, colourful, ingenious diversion, telling, in as simple or as complex a manner as required, the story of Marigold's rescue.

(NB: In the original production an animated cartoon film was used. The storyline changed a little in that Marigold proved too large to fit in Jack's rocket. So he took Beep and Buzz's spaceship; Beep and Buzz chased after on a space motorbike. This meant, of course, that Marigold's return in the next scene was from the spaceship, not the rocket, which was technically easier.)

SCENE 7

*The Farmyard*

*Exactly as we left it, with everyone staring up into the sky. Cheers as the rocket lands*

    *More cheers as the hatch opens and Marigold steps out, followed by Jack*

*Mrs Macdonald and Jeannie and Dog rush to welcome them*

**Song 10B: Marigold** (Reprise)

**All**                        Welcome home, Marigold
                              Never more to be sold
                              Marigold, Marigold,

> Welcome home today
> Welcome home to stay.

*The music continues*

**Mrs Macdonald** Well done, Jack Mac! If you hadn't had your head in the clouds, we'd never have had Marigold back, we'd never still have our farm, and we'd never have had such an exciting adventure. (*Affectionately hugging him*) You great pudd'n'! (*To the audience*) But we mustn't forget our visitors! Have you enjoyed yourselves?
**Audience** (*hopefully*) Yes.
**Mrs Macdonald** Good. Any time you want to come back, you'll be welcome—at ...
**All** Mrs Macdonald's Farm!

### Song 10C: Mrs Macdonald's Farm (Reprise)

*All join in the appropriate parts, including the audience*

| | |
|---|---|
| **Mrs Macdonald** | I'm Mrs Macdonald |
| | And this is my farm |
| **All** | E I E I O |
| **Mrs Macdonald** | And on my farm I have a cow— |

*Fanfare. Marigold does a triumphant dance*

| | |
|---|---|
| **All** | E I E I O |
| | With a (*moo moo*) here |
| | A (*moo moo*) there |
| | Here a (*moo*) |
| | There a (*moo*) |
| | Ev'rywhere a (*moo*) |

*Dog comes forward*

| | |
|---|---|
| | With a (*bark bark*) here |
| | A (*bark bark*) there |
| | Here a (*bark*) |
| | There a (*bark*) |
| | Ev'rywhere a (*bark*) |
| **Mrs Macdonald** | I'm Mrs Macdonald |
| | And this is my farm |
| **All** | E I E I O. |

---

### OPTIONAL

| | |
|---|---|
| **Mrs Macdonald** | I'm Mrs Macdonald |
| | And this is my farm |
| **All** | E I E I O |
| **Mrs Macdonald** | And on my farm I have a daughter |

*Fanfare. Jeannie comes forward and does a few karate chops*

**All**            E I E I O.

With a chop chop here
A chop chop there
Here a chop
There a chop
Ev'rywhere a chop
With a (*moo moo*) here
A (*moo moo*) there
Here a (*moo*)
There a (*moo*)
Ev'rywhere a (*moo*)
With a (*bark bark*) here
A (*bark bark*) there
Here a (*bark*)
There a (*bark*)
Ev'rywhere a (*bark*)

**Mrs Macdonald**    I'm Mrs Macdonald
And this is my farm

**All**            E I E I O.

**Mrs Macdonald**    I'm Mrs Macdonald
And this is my farm

**All**            E I E I O.

**Mrs Macdonald**    And on my farm I've ducks and pigs

*The Ducks and Pigs come forward and do a little dance*

*For the noises, everyone points from one group to the other*

**All**            E I E I O
With a (*quack quack*) here
A (*snort snort*) there
Here a (*quack*)
There a (*snort*)
Ev'rywhere a (*quack/snort*)
With a chop chop here
A chop chop there
Here a chop
There a chop
Ev'rywhere a chop
With a (*moo moo*) here
A (*moo moo*) there
Here a (*moo*)
There a (*moo*)
Ev'rywhere a (*moo*)
With a (*bark bark*) here
A (*bark bark*) there
Here a (*bark*)
There a (*bark*)
Ev'rywhere a (*bark*)

| | |
|---|---|
| **Mrs Macdonald** | I'm Mrs Macdonald |
| | And this is my farm |
| **All** | E I E I O. |

---

| | |
|---|---|
| **Mrs Macdonald** | I'm Mrs Macdonald |
| | And this is my farm |
| **All** | E I E I O |
| **Mrs Macdonald** | And on my farm I have a son |

*Fanfare. Jack steps forward. He mimes his rocket*

| | |
|---|---|
| **All** | E I E I O |
| **Jack** | With a whoosh whoosh here |
| | A whoosh whoosh there |
| | Here a whoosh |
| | There a whoosh |
| | Ev'rywhere a whoosh |
| **All** | With a (*quack quack*) here |
| | A (*snort snort*) there |
| | Here a (*quack*) |
| | There a (*snort*) |
| | Ev'rywhere a (*quack/snort*) |
| | With a chop chop here |
| | A chop chop there |
| | Here a chop |
| | There a chop |
| | Ev'rywhere a chop |
| | With a (*moo moo*) here |
| | A (*moo moo*) there |
| | Here a (*moo*) |
| | There a (*moo*) |
| | Ev'rywhere a (*moo*) |
| | With a (*bark bark*) here |
| | A (*bark bark*) there |
| | Here a (*bark*) |
| | There a (*bark*) |
| | Ev'rywhere a (*bark*) |
| **Mrs Macdonald** | I'm Mrs Macdonald |
| | And this is my farm |
| **All** | E I E I O. |

CURTAIN

### Music 10D: Encore

*If a reprise is required after the curtain calls, it is suggested that "Cloud Cuckoo Land " and/or "Keep Your Pecker Up" be used*

### Music 10E: House Exit

*See vocal score for suggestions*

# FURNITURE AND PROPERTY LIST

## ACT I

### SCENE 1

*On stage:* Dog kennel
Signposts
Water pump
Water-trough
Bails of straw
Feeding trough. *Next to it:* bucket of pigswill
Basket of grain
Stool, bucket, optional list of milking instructions

*Off stage:* Bucket and mop **(Mrs Macdonald)**
Wheelbarrow full of logs **(Jeannie)**
Large sheet of paper **(Jack)**
Bent and battered bucket, blackened face **(Jack)**
Spaceship **(Stage Management)**
Silver suitcase containing screwdriver, oil can, book "The Universe A–Z",
  cards or book of animal pictures **(Buzz)**

*Personal:* **Jack:** spectacles
**Sergeant Sweet:** rule book
**Beep, Buzz:** walkie-talkies (required throughout)

### SCENE 2

*On stage:* Signpost

*Off stage:* Cow picture **(Beep** and **Buzz)**
Space vacuum cleaner **(Buzz)**

### SCENE 3

*On stage:* As end Scene 1, plus:
6 silver cylinders in spaceship
Broom

*Off stage:* Booster (open tin of beans), plate **(Jeannie)**

### SCENE 4

*On stage:* 3 beds and bedding. *In one:* boosters
Candles

SCENE 5

*On stage:* As Scene 1, plus:
Growing baked bean tin tree (operated by **Stage Management**)

SCENE 6

*On stage:* Baked bean tin tree
Clouds

# ACT II

SCENE 1

*On stage:* As ACT I, Scene 5

*Off stage:* 2 buckets, one of pigswill, one of grain **(Jeannie)**

SCENE 2

*On stage:* Huge silver gates. *On them:* silver loop for **Marigold**
Silver trees, shrubs
Top of baked bean tin tree

*Off stage:* Silver bucket **(Buzz)**

SCENE 3

*On stage:* Oversize table. *On it:* moneybags containing silver coins, money box, giant
spoon
Oversize chair
Giant baby's playpen. *On floor near it:* silver teddy
Alarm bell near door

*Off stage:* Silver bucket **(Jack)**
Club **(Silver Giant)**
Dummy on ribbon round neck, giant club rattle **(Baby Giant)**
Silver bucket **(Beep, Buzz)**

SCENE 4

*On stage:* As Scene 2

*Off stage:* Moneybags **(Jack, Jeannie, Mrs Macdonald, Dog)**

SCENE 5

*On stage:* As ACT I, Scene 5, plus:
Rocket set in shack

*Off stage:* Car or bicycle with hooter and optional songsheet **(Sergeant Sweet)**
Moneybags **(Jack, Jeannie, Mrs Macdonald, Dog)**
2 axes **(Jeannie)**
Rocket bursting out of top of shack **(Stage Management)**

*Personal*   **Sergeant Sweet:** pocket-watch
            **Jack:** 2 boosters inside shirt

SCENE 6

*On stage:*   As required (see pages 65–66)

SCENE 7

*On stage:*   As Scene 5

*Off stage:*   Rocket **(Stage Management)**

# LIGHTING PLOT

Property fittings required: flashing lights on spaceship and on Beep and Buzz, optional lamps on helmets, flashing lights on space vacuum cleaner, candles

Various simple exterior and interior settings

ACT I

*To open:* General morning light

| | | |
|---|---|---|
| *Cue* 1 | All exit various ways<br>*Pause, then increase to very bright lighting; flashing lights on spaceship as it lands* | (Page 17) |
| *Cue* 2 | Once spaceship has landed<br>*Return to previous lighting* | (Page 17) |
| *Cue* 3 | As spaceship takes off<br>*Flashing lights* | (Page 27) |
| *Cue* 4 | **Mrs Macdonald** goes inside farmhouse<br>*Bring up lighting on bedroom for Scene 4—cosy candlelight effect—candles lit* | (Page 32) |
| *Cue* 5 | **Mrs Macdonald** blows out her candle<br>*Cut candle; pause, then candle relights* | (Page 33) |
| *Cue* 6 | **Mrs Macdonald** blows out her candle<br>*Repeat Cue 5* | (Page 33) |
| *Cue* 7 | **Mrs Macdonald** blows out her candle<br>*Repeat Cue 5* | (Page 33) |
| *Cue* 8 | **Mrs Macdonald** blows out her candle<br>*Cut candle, pause, then relight* **Jack**'s *candle* | (Page 33) |
| *Cue* 9 | **Jack** blows out his candle<br>*Cut candle* | (Page 33) |
| *Cue* 10 | As Scene 5 opens<br>*Change to night lighting—exterior* | (Page 35) |
| *Cue* 11 | As Scene 6 opens and **Jack** and **Dog** climb higher<br>*Isolate* **Dog** *and* **Jack** *in follow spots* | (Page 35) |
| *Cue* 12 | As **Jack** and **Dog** reach clouds<br>*Increase lighting* | (Page 36) |

ACT II

*To open:* General exterior lighting

| | | |
|---|---|---|
| *Cue* 13 | As **Jeannie** starts to climb tree<br>*Fade lights* | (Page 41) |

| *Cue* 14 | When ready for Scene 2<br>*Bring up bright general lighting* | (Page 41) |
| *Cue* 15 | As Scene 3 opens<br>*Change to interior lighting* | (Page 46) |
| *Cue* 16 | **Mr Meany:** "Help!"<br>*Black-out* | (Page 58) |
| *Cue* 17 | **Silver Giant** (*off*): "Don't let them escape!"<br>*Bring up lights on Scene 4* | (Page 58) |
| *Cue* 18 | **Marigold** shakes her head and sadly wanders away<br>*Black-out* | (Page 60) |
| *Cue* 19 | When ready for Scene 5<br>*Bring up general exterior lighting* | (Page 60) |
| *Cue* 20 | As rocket disappears<br>*Black-out* | (Page 65) |
| *Cue* 21 | During Scene 6<br>*Lighting as required—see pages 65–66* | (Page 65) |
| *Cue* 22 | As Scene 7 opens<br>*Bring up general exterior lighting* | (Page 66) |

# EFFECTS PLOT

## ACT I

*Cue* 1   **Mrs Macdonald:** "Five, four, three, two, one——"    (Page 12)
*Explosion from shack; smoke emerges from shack*

*Cue* 2   All exit various ways; sudden lighting effect    (Page 17)
*Electronic roaring noise*

*Cue* 3   As spaceship lands    (Page 17)
*Smoke belches from its tail*

*Cue* 4   As door or hatch of spaceship opens    (Page 17)
*Whirring noise*

*Cue* 5   (*Optional*) As **Beep** twiddles tuning knob on **Buzz**    (Page 18)
*Electronic noises, interference, etc., as though he were tuning a radio*

*Cue* 6   (*Optional*) As **Buzz** and **Beep** turn on lamps in their helmets    (Page 19)
*Electronic noise*

*Cue* 7   As **Buzz** brings on space vacuum cleaner    (Page 25)
*Loud sucking noise*

*Cue* 8   **Dog** turns off lever on vacuum cleaner    (Page 25)
*Cut sucking noise*

*Cue* 9   As door or hatch of spaceship closes    (Page 27)
*Whirring noise*

*Cue* 10   As spaceship takes off    (Page 27)
*Smoke from tail, electronic roaring noise*

*Cue* 11   As Scene 6 opens    (Page 35)
*Dry ice effect beneath clouds*

## ACT II

*Cue* 12   As **Jack** and **Dog** gently push gate    (Page 41)
*Gate creaks eerily open*

*Cue* 13   **Buzz** presses alarm bell    (Page 56)
*Alarm rings out*

*Cue* 14   **Jack** goes into shack and shuts door    (Page 65)
*Pause, then sound of engine being turned over but not starting; pause, then repeat; pause, then engine turns over and bursts into life*

*Cue* 15   As rocket bursts out of top of shack    (Page 65)
*Rocket noise, smoke or dry ice*

*Cue* 16   During Scene 6    (Page 65)
*Effects as required—see pages 65–66*

MADE AND PRINTED IN GREAT BRITAIN BY
LATIMER TREND & COMPANY LTD PLYMOUTH
MADE IN ENGLAND